Read Write Inc.
FRESH START

Fresh Start Handbook

Series developed by

Ruth Miskin

OXFORD
UNIVERSITY PRESS

OXFORD
UNIVERSITY PRESS

Great Clarendon Street, Oxford, OX2 6DP,
United Kingdom

Oxford University Press is a department of the University of Oxford.
It furthers the University's objective of excellence in research, scholarship,
and education by publishing worldwide. Oxford is a registered trade mark
of Oxford University Press in the UK and in certain other countries

First published as the *Read Write Inc. 2 Handbook* by Ruth Miskin Literacy Ltd 2005

First published by Oxford University Press 2006. Revised 2009

This edition published by Oxford University Press 2011

British Library Cataloguing in Publication Data

Data available

ISBN-13: 978-0-19-833015-8

7 9 10 8

Paper used in the production of this book is a natural, recyclable product made from wood grown in sustainable forests. The manufacturing process conforms to the environmental regulations of the country of origin.

Printed in Great Britain by Bell & Bain Ltd., Glasgow

FSC www.fsc.org
MIX
Paper from
responsible sources
FSC® C007785

Contents

Introduction 1

Dear Teachers

While I was a headteacher in London I began to devise a programme that would get all students to read and write quickly and easily. The programme has now been widely used and tested and the result is *Read Write Inc.*, an inclusive literacy programme which has been hugely successful in many schools.

There are four *Read Write Inc.* programmes: *Read Write Inc. Phonics* for children in Foundation to Year 4 (P1 to P5); *Read Write Inc. Comprehension* for children in Years 2 to 4 (P3 to P5) and *Read Write Inc. Comprehension Plus* for children in Years 2 to 6 (P3 to P7) who can read very well; *Read Write Inc. Fresh Start* for students in Years 5, 6 and 7 (P6, P7 and S1/P8) or above who are currently reading below National Curriculum Level 3 (Level C/Second level - Scotland; Level 3 - Northern Ireland) and *Read Write Inc. Spelling* for children at National Curriculum Level 2a (Level B/First Level - Scotland; Level 2 - Northern Ireland; Level 2 Wales) and above.

At the core of *Read Write Inc. Fresh Start* is the vigorous teaching of synthetic phonics. Students learn the 44 common sounds in the English language and how to sound-blend words over a short period of time, alongside spelling. They then, importantly, read *Modules* with words they can sound-blend, so they get early success in reading. The more sounds they learn, the greater the range of texts they can read.

These 34 *Modules* contain carefully graded stories and non-fiction texts. They have been written by a talented author, Gill Munton. The texts are natural, fluent, amusing and importantly, age appropriate. Students really enjoy reading them and talking about the 'Find it' and 'Prove it' questions at the end of each story; comprehension is an integral element of the programme from the start.

We want students to find writing easy and enjoyable too. The writing activities in the *Modules* build upon the stories and non-fiction texts so students make the strong link between reading and writing, spelling and grammar. Students' writing skills are developed step-by-step from simple sentences to guided compositions.

For every *Module* there are accompanying texts in the *Fresh Start Anthologies* and *More Anthologies* to encourage wider reading. These can be used for further practice, library time or home reading.

Students are assessed to find their right reading level so they can be grouped by reading progress. This is key while students are learning to read - the closer the homogeneity of the group, the faster the progress.

One of the most important things I learned in my teaching career was that students remember a lot of what they are taught if they talk about it. So partner work, involving all students talking to their partner about what they read and learn, is a crucial part of *Read Write Inc. Fresh Start*.

The overarching aim of this programme is to help schools become read-a-lot schools and talk-a-lot schools. Of course, this takes enthusiasm and relentlessness. However, it is only when all students in a school have a voice - and can read - that they can be really successful!

Ruth Miskin

Read Write Inc. Fresh Start

Reading opens the door to all learning.

A student who reads a lot will become a good reader.
A good reader will be able to read challenging material.
A student who reads challenging material is a student who will learn.
The more a student learns, the more he or she will want to find out.

The *Read Write Inc. Fresh Start* programme enables every student to become a confident and fluent reader at the first attempt.

- England: It is for students reading below NC Level 3 in Years 5, 6 and 7 who have the potential to achieve NC Level 4.
- Scotland: It is for students reading below Level C/Second Level in P6, P7 and S1 who have the potential to achieve Level D/Second Level.
- Northern Ireland: It is for students reading below Level 3 in P6, P7 and P8 who have the potential to achieve Level 4.

It is also suitable for children in older year groups who have been 'invited' to take part.

This handbook provides you with step-by-step guidance, enabling you to teach students to read and write using a simple, logical method. The students learn:

- to read effortlessly so that they can put all their energy into comprehending what they read
- to spell effortlessly so that they can put all their energy into composing what they write

Reading

The students:

- learn 44 sounds and the corresponding letters/letter groups using simple picture prompts
- learn to read words using 'Sound Talk' (sound blending)
- read lively texts featuring words they have learned to sound out
- show that they comprehend the stories by answering questions

Writing

The students:

- learn to write the letters/letter groups which represent the 44 sounds
- learn to write words by saying the sounds in 'Sound Talk'
- write simple sentences
- compose stories based on picture strips
- deconstruct and compose texts in a range of genres

Fresh Start resources

Phonics (Speed Sounds)

- Speed Sounds Cards Sets 1, 2 and 3
- Simple and Complex Speed Sounds Posters
- Green Word Cards
- Red Word Cards
- Picture-Sound Cards
- Magnetic Sounds Cards

Modules

Introductory Module

Modules 1–33

Anthologies and *More Anthologies*

- Volumes 1–7

Fourteen colour anthologies containing non-fiction, poetry and fiction texts, including quizzes, playscripts and comic strips. The *Anthologies* and *More Anthologies* texts are linked to the *Module* texts via the sounds and graphemes practised and via the content so that students meet familiar vocabulary to support their independent reading.

- *Fresh Start Handbook*

- Speed Sounds CD-ROM
  for all interactive whiteboards

The *Read Write Inc. Fresh Start Handbook*

This provides clear guidance for teachers, teaching assistants and parents on how to teach students to read and write. It should be used alongside the phonic resources and the *Modules*.
The phonics lesson plans in the handbook teach students how to read and write sounds and words.

The phonic resources

The 44 sounds and corresponding letters/letter groups (graphemes) are taught as three sets of Speed Sounds.

Speed Sounds

Speed Sounds Set 1
m a s d t i n p g o c
k u b f e l h sh r j v y
w th z ch qu x ng nk

Speed Sounds Set 2
ay ee igh ow oo oo ar
or air ir ou oy

Speed Sounds Set 3
ea oi a-e i-e o-e u-e aw are ur
er ow ai oa ew ire ear
ure cious tious tion

There are three sets of phonic lessons for the Speed Sounds, each with its own set of phonic resources.

Set 1

Speed Sounds Set 1 and sound-blending must be taught before the students read any *Modules*.
Once they have been taught Set 1 sounds and sound-blending, they will begin to read the *Modules*.
Speed Sounds Set 1 are contained in the Introductory Module and *Modules* 1–3.
Only when they are secure on all of Set 1 sounds will students begin to learn Set 2.

Speed Sounds Cards: Set 1 m a s d t i n p g o c k u b f e l h sh r j v y w th z ch qu x ng nk and Simple Speed Sounds Poster	Letter-sound pictures are used to help students learn the sounds quickly, e.g. a picture of a dinosaur is 'morphed' into the letter 'd'. 
Green Word Cards	These cards feature the above graphemes (letters/letter groups) and are used for sound-blending practice.
Red Word Cards	Students learn to read a few words that cannot be read easily by sound blending. These words are taught as students read the texts.

Introduction 1

Set 2

Well before students read *Module* 4 they begin to learn Speed Sounds Set 2. They continue to accumulate the Set 2 phonic knowledge and blending ability required for each *Module* before they read the text. Speed Sounds Sets 1 and 2 are contained in *Modules* 4–13. Only when they are secure on all of Set 2 sounds will students begin to learn Set 3.

Simple and Complex Speed Sounds Posters	This features all the graphemes that students are taught throughout the *Fresh Start* programme. It is used in every *Module* lesson.
Speed Sounds Cards: Set 2 ay ee igh ow oo oo ar or air ir ou oy	A phrase and a picture help students to read each of these long vowel sounds, e.g. 'm**ay** I pl**ay**?'  ay
Green Word Cards	These cards feature the above graphemes and are used for sound-blending practice.
Red Word Cards	Students learn to read a few words that cannot be read easily by sound blending. These words are taught as students read the texts.

Set 3

Well before students read *Module* 14 they begin to learn Speed Sounds Set 3. They continue to accumulate the Set 3 phonic knowledge and blending ability required for each *Module* well before they read the text. Speed Sounds Sets 1, 2 and 3 are contained in *Modules* 14–33.

Complex Speed Sounds Poster	This features all the graphemes that students are taught throughout the *Fresh Start* programme. It is used in every *Module* lesson.
Speed Sounds Cards: Set 3 ea oi a-e i-e o-e u-e aw are ur er ow ai oa ew ire ear ure cious tious tion	A phrase and a picture help students to read each of these long vowel sounds, e.g. 'm**a**k**e** a c**a**k**e**', 'ph**o**n**e** h**o**m**e**', 'n**i**c**e** sm**i**l**e**', 'cup of t**ea**'.  ea
Green Word Cards	These cards feature the above graphemes and are used for sound-blending practice.
Red Word Cards	Students learn to read a few words that cannot be read easily by sound blending. These words are taught as students read the texts.

The *Modules*

The *Modules* contain fiction and non-fiction texts and a range of activities which develop students' reading, writing, spelling and comprehension skills. (See page 40.)

The phonic knowledge required for each *Module* is taught before the text is read; the students are prepared for every text so they have early success in reading.

The texts have been written by Gill Munton, a talented and experienced author. When you read Gill's stories and non-fiction texts, you forget that you are reading a text with a strong phonic structure. The language is natural and fluent, each text has a clear shape, and humour is a strong feature – so students want to read the books again and again.

The *Anthologies*

The *Fresh Start Anthologies* and *More Anthologies* provide extra practice of the sounds and graphemes focused on in the *Modules* through a variety of lively texts to encourage students to read for pleasure. (See page 50.)

National Curriculum reading levels

Approximate NC level for reading if decoding well and understanding texts	Scotland: Curriculum for Excellence	Northern Ireland Curriculum	Modules completed	Speed Sounds known effortlessly and blending
1c-1b	Early	Level 1	Introductory	Set 1
1b-1a	Early	Level 1	1-3	Set 1
1a-2b	Early	Level 1/2	4-13	Sets 1 + 2
2b-3b	Early/First	Level 2/3	14-20	Sets 1, 2 + 3 (oi, a-e, ea, i-e, ie, o-e, u-e, ue, aw, au)
3b-4c/b	First/ Second	Level 3/4	21-33	Sets 1, 2 + 3 (are, ur, er, ow, ai, aigh, eigh, o-e, oa, u-e, ue, ew plus endings: -le, -il, -al, -ent, -ence, -ant, -ance, -ture, -ure, -our, -or, -ous, -ious, -cious, -tious, -able, -ably, -ible, -ibly, -tion, -sion, -ssion)

Roles and responsibilities

The headteacher

Read Write Inc. Fresh Start works best with the full commitment of the senior management team. One member should attend the initial training sessions, and provide cover for at least three hours a week so that the manager of the programme can ensure it is implemented to the highest standards in all classes.

The *Read Write Inc. Fresh Start* manager

The manager will be a senior member of staff, responsible for:

- supporting teachers in the implementation of *Read Write Inc. Fresh Start*
- planning 'hotlist' sessions with the 1-to-1 ten-minute tutors (see below)
- spotting students with poor attendance
- diagnosing reading problems with the 1-to-1 ten-minute teachers

The *Read Write Inc. Fresh Start* teachers

It is vital that teachers are selected because they are considered by students and staff to be 'high status' teachers and can maintain a high level of positive discipline.Teachers are responsible for teaching groups of students who have been organised homogeneously according to reading level. It is the teacher's responsibility to notify the manager of any student whose progress is either faster or slower than that of the rest of the group. The manager should act on this information as quickly as possible.

The *Read Write Inc. Fresh Start* 1-to-1 ten-minute tutors

The manager compiles a 'hotlist' of the small number of students who, for whatever reason, have great difficulty in making progress in reading, even in a small group. The 1-to-1 ten-minute tutors support these students individually for just 10-15 minutes a day until they can do the following:

Priority 1: read Set 1 of the Speed Sounds Cards effortlessly
Priority 2: read the Green Word Cards (Set 1) by sound blending
Priority 3: read the *Modules* at the same pace as the rest of their group

Priority is always given to reading; teachers must focus on the students' reading ability rather than their writing ability at this early stage.

2 Organising *Read Write Inc. Fresh Start* in your school

Training

The manager, teachers, assistants and tutors receive two days' intensive training. Cascade training is not used.

Length of time needed

Students will need to spend a full hour each day on the programme. Please allow extra time for movement around the school.

Assessment

Assess students' reading using the *Read Write Inc. Fresh Start* Entry Test (see Section 6). This will help you to group the students homogeneously and decide where in the programme each group should start.

Once the programme has started, students who make faster or slower progress than the rest of the group should be identified quickly, so re-grouping can occur straight away.

The manager must know of every student who is making slow progress. If only one or two students in a group are in this category, the manager must consider putting them on the 'hotlist'. If there are more than a few of these students, it is likely that the teacher needs further support.

For Ongoing Assessment see page 63.

Grouping

If the students in each group are closely matched in terms of ability, the teaching will be more focused and progress will be faster.

Read Write Inc. Fresh Start is intended for three different groups of children:

- Students who are reading at or below NC level 2a (Level B/First level - Scotland; Level 2 - Northern Ireland) before they start on the programme, but have the potential to achieve well – if only they had fluent reading and writing skills.
- Students who consider themselves to be good readers but have poor comprehension and writing skills; they are generally working at NC level 2b–3c (approximately Level B/First level - Scotland; Level 2 - Northern Ireland).
- Students with fundamental learning difficulties reading at or below NC level 2a (Level B/First level - Scotland; Level 2 - Northern Ireland).

These groups should be taught separately; each will start at a different point, work at a different pace, and the teacher will put a greater stress on either reading or writing.

Students who are predicted to make fast progress can be taught in groups of 12–16, whereas students who have learning difficulties as well as low reading ability should work in much smaller groups. The management will need to consider the timetabling implications. It is important that students are willing participants in the programme. They may not be so willing if they have to be withdrawn from favourite lessons such as P.E. and art.

Homework

It is helpful if parents and carers support students' reading at home. Once the students are halfway through *Read Write Inc. Fresh Start*, they will be bringing home other books which have been introduced in class and which they can read for themselves. This is vital so that students read a wide variety of books through the year.

Attendance

The programme is intensive and cumulative, so poor attendance will severely disrupt a student's progress. A teacher should arrange to meet the parents of those students who have both poor attendance and low reading ability. It may help if these parents are phoned at 9.00 a.m. if the student is late or absent. A suggested letter to parents for you to adapt as necessary is provided below.

Dear Mr and Mrs Smith,

Tom's reading

Tom has been selected to take part in a very intensive reading and writing course. This course will, however, only be successful if:

1 Tom comes to school **every** day at 9.00, unless he is very poorly.

2 He behaves well and shows a commitment to learning to read. He must understand that he will be removed from the course if his behaviour causes us concern. However, no other provision will be made to support Tom's reading if this happens.

Please could you sign the form below if you agree to Tom taking part in this course.

Mrs Jones, the reading manager would like to meet you to discuss all the work we are about to do with Tom on 3rd May at 3.15.

Best wishes

Headteacher

....

I agree that Tom may attend the reading and writing course.
I agree to help Tom by making sure he arrives at school every day at 9.00.
I understand that Tom will be removed from the course if his behaviour causes concern.

Mr and Mrs Smith

Planning and preparation

Once you have read this handbook and taught a few lessons, you will have very little preparation to do before each lesson. You will need to:

- get to know the *Module*
- read the teacher's notes in the *Module*
- write the green, challenge and vocabulary words on the board

Partner work

Partner work is a crucial element of the programme.

We learn:

- 10% of what we read
- 20% of what we see
- 30% of what we hear
- 50% of what we see and hear
- 70% of what we discuss with another person
- 85% of what we experience personally
- 95% of what we teach

(*William Glasser*)

We learn 70% of what we discuss with another person

If we want all students to take a full part in all lessons, all students should answer every question. There should be nowhere for any student to 'hide' in any lesson. Working in pairs facilitates this.

Responsibility for talking should not be an optional extra; we should expect students to talk in the same way as we expect them to write and read.

We learn 95% of what we teach

To take Glasser's research to its ultimate conclusion, to teach gives mastery. In order to teach something, we must analyse and organise our ideas so that somebody else can understand them. Working in pairs, students are taught to teach and support each other to read, comprehend, spell and write their own compositions.

The students must know that they will all be expected to:

- answer every question
- practise every activity with their partner
- take turns in teaching each other

Partner work (continued)

Choosing partnerships

In all circumstances, the teacher decides on the partnerships. Partnerships should be chosen with care, and rotated every few weeks.

- Pair a 'lively' student with an assertive, well-behaved student.
- Pair two dominating students. (They can take turns to listen.)
- Pair two shy students. (Someone has to talk!)
- Mix boys and girls, levels of maturity, and first and second language learners as much as possible.

If there is a student who is particularly difficult, choose his or her partner carefully. Explain privately to the partner why he or she has been chosen, how much you appreciate his or her patience, and how hard you expect him or her to work. Be wary of over-using the same student to partner more challenging students.

Try to avoid odd numbers, but if this is unavoidable, make up a three.

Learning to work in a partnership

When students start to work in partnerships, it is important to establish good working relationships. Students need to understand that they do not have to be best friends with their partners in order to work with them in a civil manner. Make sure they all know that they will have the opportunity to partner lots of different students during other lessons. Discuss how they will feel if they are asked to work with someone they don't like (without mentioning names). See Appendix F for partnership warm-up exercises.

Show appropriate and inappropriate partner behaviour through role play.

Ask students to work in partnerships in activities outside the *Read Write Inc. Fresh Start* sessions.

There will always be one or two students who find partner work challenging. However, they must understand that you will be relentless in establishing this way of working. It may be difficult to institute partner work, but never give up. Your efforts will pay dividends later.

(Ways to collect partnership responses are listed in Appendix G.)

3 Organising *Read Write Inc. Fresh Start* in your classroom

Managing the group

Remember: participation, positive teaching, pace, purpose and passion.

Students enjoy learning to read and write (and therefore learn more successfully) when these principles become embedded in your teaching.

Participation

All students are expected to participate in every lesson. If a question is worth asking, it's worth answering. If an activity is worth doing, it's worth doing well. Develop a 'Good partner' chart with the students (see Appendix E - good partner chart.)

Positive teaching

Students learn much more quickly in an assertive and positive climate. They talk more readily in an atmosphere free of anger and tension. Shouting, nagging and 'shushing' have a detrimental effect on students' talking and therefore on their learning.

Catch them being good! Use *praise actions* to keep the students energetic and to praise excellent behaviour and hard work. Examples: high five/thumbs up; fireworks and whooshes (act out); Go guys! (circle thumbs); Elvis (thank you, thank you, thank you very much – push hand through hair); marshmallow claps (squishy clap); microwaves (little finger waves).

Students want to please us, so praise them explicitly for specific things. Teachers know their students: some students prefer quiet, private praise, while others are happy for it to be shared with the group. Praise them, in particular, for their partner work. As they overhear the explicit praise, others will copy the good partner behaviour. (See Appendix E for positive teaching.)

Pace

A brisk pace is essential. Students should be working so hard that they do not have any 'down time'. If the pace is too slow, students become restless and there is more potential for challenging behaviour to start. If any lethargy steps in, ask everyone to stop and stretch for ten seconds. Open the windows!

Purpose

Every part of a lesson has a specific purpose. It is important to keep that purpose clearly in your mind as you teach.

Passion

This is a very prescriptive programme, which is why it works so well. However, it is the energy, enthusiasm and passion that teachers put into the lessons that bring the teaching and learning to life. Pedestrian teaching will not have the same impact as passionate teaching!

Managing the group (continued)

Management signals

Use your voice for teaching, not classroom management. The following signals will make your teaching easier and more effective, particularly if they are adopted by the whole school.

- **The 'my turn, your turn' signal**

There are times in the programme when you will need the students to copy what you do.

My turn: touch your chest with your palm when it's your turn.
Your turn: open your palm to the students when it's their turn.

- **The 'stop' signal**

When all the students are answering every question, you must be able to gain their attention quickly and easily, without the need to raise your voice.

Hold your hand up in the air. Do not talk while the hand is raised. The students then finish what they are saying, raise their hands in response, and check that others have seen the signal, gently tapping an arm if necessary (avoiding poking with elbows and saying 'oi'.) Do not start talking until everyone has returned the signal. If the signal fails, lower your hand and remind the students of the school's expectations. Explain that all the adults in the school will be using the stop signal. The students must return the signal to any adult who uses it.

- **The 'turn to your partner' signal (TTYP)**

While you establish 'TTYP', tap two fingers together to warn the students, before you ask a question, that they will need to turn to their partners to answer.

Explain that the 'hands up' system for answering questions will not be used. (However, 'hands up' for clarification and for asking further questions should be encouraged.)

- **The 'perfect partner position' signal**

When working together, partners should sit side by side and shoulder to shoulder. (If they face each other, the noise level increases.) They position the book so that both partners can see it. Partner 1 points to the first sound/word and Partner 2 gets ready to read.

When you say 'Go', Partner 2 keeps reading until you raise your hand. (The students should never say 'I've finished', but should practise until you raise your hand.)

The partners then reverse roles.

Phonic lessons for students

There are three sets of phonic lessons.

Set 1 phonic lessons are taught before the *Module* lessons begin.
Students are taught to read and write the following graphemes and to read words containing them by sound blending.

m a s d t i n p g o c k u b f e l h sh r j v y w th z ch qu x ng nk

Set 2 phonic lessons are taught alongside the *Introductory Module and Modules 1-13*. Students are taught to read and write the following graphemes and to read words containing them by sound blending.

ay ee igh ow oo *oo* ar or air ir ou oy

Set 3 phonic lessons are taught alongside books 14–33 of the *Modules*. Students are taught to read and write alternative graphemes representing the vowel sounds already taught in Set 2, and some common word endings.

a-e i-e o-e u-e ea aw are ur er ow ai oa ew ire ear ure tious cious tion

Set 1 phonic lessons

Set 1 Speed Sounds are taught in groups in this order:

m a s d t
i n p g o
c k u b
f e l h sh
r j v y w
th z ch qu x ng nk

Blending lessons

Once students know a group of sounds they:

- make words with magnetic letters for reading and spelling
- read the corresponding Green Word Cards in Sound Talk (sound blending)
- spell the words using Sound Fingers (finger spelling)

The Set 1 Speed Sounds are either stretchy or bouncy.

Stretchy sounds: m s f l sh r v w th z ng nk
Bouncy sounds: a d t i n p g o c k u b e h j y ch qu x

The phonic lessons 4

Use the 'm' blueprint lesson for all the stretchy sounds and the 'a' blueprint lesson for all the bouncy sounds. Aim to teach three new sounds a day.

You will need:

- Speed Sounds Cards (Set 1)
- Simple Speed Sounds Chart
- A few objects whose names start with each of the sounds and/or the Picture-Sound Cards
- Green Word Cards (Set 1) displayed on a 'Green Word Wall'
- Magnetic Sound Cards

Once you have taught the sounds m a s d t teach Blending Lesson 1 (see page 21).
The chart below shows the order in which to teach Speed Sounds Set 1 and the blending lessons that should follow the teaching of each group:

m	a	s	d	t	then Blending Lesson 1
i	n	p	g	o	then Blending Lesson 2
c	k	u	b		then Blending Lesson 3
f	e	l	h	sh	then Blending Lesson 4
r	j	v	y	w	then Blending Lesson 5
th	z	ch	qu		
x	ng	nk			then Blending Lessons 6 and 7
					then keep practising the sounds previously taught.

The *Speed Sounds Lesson Plans* book provides detailed teaching notes for teaching each sound, should you require more guidance.

• Blueprint lesson plan for 'm' and other stretchy sounds

Say m

1 Stretch mmmmmm as you press your lips together hard.

2 Hold up the Picture-Sound cards of the mouse, mirror, mountain and moon, in turn. (Or for other stretchy sounds select the Picture-Sound cards with pictures with the appropriate initial sound.)
Stretch the sound at the start as you say the name of each picture:
mmmmouse, mmmmirror, mmmmountain, mmmmoon.
Now ask the students to say the name of each picture, mixing them up until the students are fluent.

Read m

1 Copy Maisie and the mountains onto the board.
Run your finger down Maisie and then over the two mountains, saying mmm.
Say mountain as you touch the end of the second mountain.

2 Write m on the board beside Maisie and the mountains. Make it the same size.
Run your finger down and then over m, saying mmm.
Say m just as you touch the end of m.
Repeat 1 and 2 several times.

praise constantly!

3 Show the Speed Sounds card (picture side). Say mountain.
Show the letter side. Say m. Repeat until students are fluent.

4 Find it on the Simple Speed Sounds chart.

Write m

1 Handwrite
Air-write m, saying: Maisie, mountain, mountain as you go down Maisie and then over the two mountains.

2 Sound-write
Stretch mmmmm, in a rhythm, as you air-write a large m.
Repeat 1 and 2, getting faster each time.
Repeat 1 and 2 on paper.

Sound Talk (oral)

1 Say these words in Sound Talk:
m-a-n, m-u-m, m-a-d, m-u-d, j-a-m.

2 Students repeat the Sound Talk and say the word.
m-a-n man, m-u-m mum, m-a-d mad, m-u-d mud,
j-a-m jam

practise Sound Talk frequently, using other one-syllable words

Blueprint lesson plan for 'a' and other bouncy sounds

Say a

1. Bounce a-a-a-a. Open your mouth wide, as if to take a big bite of an apple.
2. Hold up the Picture-Sound cards of the apple, ant, astronaut and acrobat, in turn. (Or for other bouncy sounds select the Picture-Sound cards with pictures with the appropriate initial sound.)
   Bounce the sound at the start as you say the name of each picture:
   a-a-a-apple, a-a-a-ant, a-a-a-astronaut, a-a-a-acrobat.
   Now ask the students to say the name of each picture, mixing them up until the students are fluent.

Read a

1. Copy the apple onto the board.
   Run your finger round the apple, saying a-a-a-a.
   Say apple as you touch the leaf of the apple.
2. Write a on the board beside the apple. Make it the same size.
   Run your finger round a, saying a-a-a-a.
   Say a just as you touch the end of a.
   Repeat 1 and 2 several times.
3. Show the Speed Sounds card (picture side). Say apple.
   Show the letter side. Say a.
   Repeat until students are fluent.
4. Find it on the Simple Speed Sounds chart.

★ praise constantly! ★

Write a

1. Handwrite
   Air-write a, saying: round the apple, down the leaf.
2. Sound-write
   Bounce a-a-a-a, in a rhythm, as you air-write a large a.
   Repeat 1 and 2, getting faster each time.
   Repeat 1 and 2 on paper.

Speed Write

Say mmmmm, a-a-a-a, as students write the sounds.

Sound Talk (oral)

1. Say these words in Sound Talk, emphasising a:
   m-a-n, m-a-d, h-a-m, j-a-m, S-a-m.
2. Students repeat the Sound Talk and say the word.
   m-a-n man, m-a-d mad, h-a-m ham, j-a-m jam, S-a-m Sam

★ practise Sound Talk frequently, using other one-syllable words ★

Review

Start building up a pack of Speed Sounds cards made up of the Speed Sounds students know. Use it to review the Speed Sounds speedily in each lesson. Check all students know the sounds. Commence additional one-to-one tutoring for any student who is struggling.

Blending Lesson 1

To be taught after students have been taught m, a, s, d, t.

> it is vital that you avoid saying 'uh' at the end of each sound - KEEP THE SOUNDS PURE!

Step 1: Speed read the sounds
Practise reading m, a, s, d, t in and out of order at speed.

Step 2: Sound Talk to read
Give partners one magnetic board and magnetic letters m, a, s, d, t.

Put the Speed Sound cards m, a, t in your pocket chart close together.
Point to each card as you say the sounds.
Say the word, sweeping your pointer from left to right under the word.

Repeat a few times saying the sounds and then the word with the students.
Repeat with: mat, sad, dad, sat, at.

Silently, make m - a - t on the board with the Speed Sounds cards. Ask partner 1s to:
put magnetic letters m, a, t on their magnetic boards;
point to each letter and say the sounds to partner 2;
say the word to partner 2.
Repeat with: mad, sad, dad, sat, at.
Partners take turns at being the 'teacher' – making the words.
N.B. First check that at least one partner can sound-blend. Support partners who have difficulty.

Find Green Word cards 1.1.
Point to the sounds as they read the words in Sound Talk.
Display the word in a pocket chart and return to practise.

Step 3: Sound Fingers to spell
Say: Show me three fingers.
Say the word: mat.
Model how you touch each finger firmly as you say the sounds: m-a-t.
Model writing the word on the board.

Say the word: mat.
Ask the students to press the sounds on their fingers.
Ask the students to write the word.
Ask them to say the word in sounds as they write.
Repeat with: mad, sad, dad, sat, at.

Blending Lesson 1 should be repeated as i, n, p, g, o are being taught.

Blending Lesson 2

To be taught after students have been taught i, n, p, g, o.

> it is vital that you avoid saying 'uh' at the end of each sound - KEEP THE SOUNDS PURE!

Step 1: Speed read the sounds

Practise reading m, a, s, d, t, i, n, p, g, o in and out of order at speed.

Step 2: Sound Talk to read

Give partners one magnetic board and magnetic letters m a s d t i n p g o.
Put the Speed Sound cards d, o, g in your pocket chart close together.
Point to each card as you say the sounds.
Say the word, sweeping your pointer from left to right under the word.

Repeat a few times saying the sounds and then the word with the students.
Repeat with six of these words: in on it an and pin got dog sit tip pan gap dig top.

Silently, make d - o - g on the board with the Speed Sounds cards. Ask partner 1s to:
put letters d, o, g on their magnetic boards;
point to each letter and say the sounds to partner 2;
say the word to partner 2.
Ask partners to repeat with six words.
Partners take turns at being the 'teacher' – making the words.
N.B. First check that at least one partner can sound-blend. Support partners who have difficulty.

Find Green Word cards 1.2.
Point to the sounds as they read the words in Sound Talk.
Display the word in a pocket chart and return to practise.

Step 3: Sound Fingers to spell

Say: Show me three fingers.
Say the word: dog.
Model how you touch each finger firmly as you say the sounds: d-o-g.
Model writing the word on the board.

Say the word: dog.
Ask the students to press the sounds on their fingers.
Ask the students to write the word.
Ask them to say the word in sounds as they write.
Repeat with a few words.

Blending Lesson 2 should be repeated as c, k, u, b are being taught.

Blending Lesson 3

> ★ it is vital that you avoid saying 'uh' at the end of each sound - KEEP THE SOUNDS PURE! ★

To be taught after students have been taught c, k, u, b.

Step 1: Speed read the sounds

Practise reading m, a, s, d, t, i, n, p, g, o, c, k, u, b in and out of order at speed.

Step 2: Sound Talk to read

Give partners one magnetic board and magnetic letters m, a, s, d, t, i, n, p, g, o, c, k, u, b.
Put the Speed Sound cards c, a, t in your pocket chart close together.
Point to each card as you say the sounds.
Say the word, sweeping your pointer from left to right under the word.

Repeat a few times saying the sounds and then the word with the students.
Repeat with six of these words: bin cat cot can kit mud up cup bad back kick pick.

Silently, make c - a - t on the board with the Speed Sounds cards. Ask partner 1s to:
put letters c, a, t on their magnetic boards;
point to each letter and say the sounds to partner 2;
say the word to partner 2.
Ask partners to repeat with six words.
Partners take turns at being the 'teacher' - making the words.
N.B. First check that at least one partner can sound-blend. Support partners who have difficulty.

Find Green Word cards 1.3.
Point to the sounds as they read the words in Sound Talk.
Display the word in a pocket chart and return to practise.

Step 3: Sound Fingers to spell

Say: Show me three fingers.
Say the word: cat.
Model how you touch each finger firmly as you say the sounds: c-a-t.
Model writing the word on the board.

Say the word: cat.
Ask the students to press the sounds on their fingers.
Ask the students to write the word.
Ask them to say the word in sounds as they write.
Repeat with a few words.

Blending Lesson 3 should be repeated as f, e, l, h, sh are being taught.

Blending Lesson 4

To be taught after students have been taught f, e, l, h, sh.

> it is vital that you avoid saying 'uh' at the end of each sound - KEEP THE SOUNDS PURE!

Step 1: Speed read the sounds

Practise reading m, a, s, d, t, i, n, p, g, o, c, k, ck, u, b, f, e, l, h, sh in and out of order at speed.

Step 2: Sound Talk to read

Give partners one magnetic board and magnetic letters m a s d t i n p g o c k ck u b f e l h sh.

Put the Speed Sound cards f, i, sh in your pocket chart close together.
Point to each card as you say the sounds.
Say the word, sweeping your pointer from left to right under the word.

Repeat a few times saying the sounds and then the word with the students.
Repeat with six of these words: met set fan fun fat lip log let had hit hen ship shop sack.

Silently make f - i - sh on the board with the Speed Sounds cards. Ask partner 1s to:
put letters f, i, sh on their magnetic boards;
point to each letter and say the sounds to partner 2;
say the word to partner 2.

Ask partners to repeat with six words.
Parters take turns at being the 'teacher' – making the words.
N.B. First check that at least one partner can sound-blend. Support partners who have difficulty.

Find Green Word cards 1.4.
Point to the sounds as they read the words in Sound Talk.
Display the word in a pocket chart and return to practise.

Step 3: Sound Fingers to spell

Say: Show me three fingers.
Say the word: fish.
Model how you touch each finger firmly as you say the sounds: f-i-sh.
Model writing the word on the board.

Say the word: fish.
Ask the students to press the sounds on their fingers.
Ask the students to write the word.
Ask them to say the word in sounds as they write.
Repeat with a few words.

Blending Lesson 4 should be repeated as r, j, v, y, w are being taught.

Blending Lesson 5

To be taught after students have been taught r, j, v, y, w.

it is vital that you avoid saying 'uh' at the end of each sound - KEEP THE SOUNDS PURE!

Step 1: Speed read the sounds

Practise reading m, a, s, d, t, i, n, p, g, o, c, k, ck, u, b, f, e, l, h, sh, r, j, v, y, w in and out of order at speed.

Step 2: Sound Talk to read

Give partners one magnetic board and magnetic letters m a s d t i n p g o c k ck u b f e l h sh r j v y w.
Put the Speed Sound cards w, e, t in your pocket chart close together.
Point to each card as you say the sounds.
Say the word, sweeping your pointer from left to right under the word.

Repeat a few times saying the sounds and then the word with the children.
Repeat with six of these words: red run rat jog jet jam vet yap yes yum web win wish sock.

Silently make w - e - t on the board with the Speed Sounds cards. Ask partner 1s to:
put letters w, e, t on their magnetic boards;
point to each letter and say the sounds to partner 2;
say the word to partner 2.
Ask partners to repeat with six words.
Partners take turns at being the 'teacher' - making the words.
N.B. First check that at least one partner can sound-blend. Support partners who have difficulty.

Find Green Word cards 1.5.
Point to the sounds as they read the words in Sound Talk.
Display the word in a pocket chart and return to practise.

Step 3: Sound Fingers to spell

Say: Show me three fingers.
Say the word: wet.
Model how you touch each finger firmly as you say the sounds: w-e-t.
Model writing the word on the board.

Say the word: wet.
Ask the students to press the sounds on their fingers.
Ask the students to write the word.
Ask them to say the word in sounds as they write.
Repeat with a few words.

Blending Lesson 5 should be repeated as th, z, ch, qu, x, ng, nk are being taught.

Blending Lesson 6

To be taught after students have been taught th, z, ch, qu, x, ng, nk.

> it is vital that you avoid saying 'uh' at the end of each sound - KEEP THE SOUNDS PURE!

Step 1: Speed read the sounds

Practise reading m, a, s, d, t, i, n, p, g, o, c, k, ck, u, b, f, e, l, h, sh, r, j, v, y, w, th, z, ch, qu, x, ng, nk in and out of order at speed.

Step 2: Sound Talk to read

Give partners one magnetic board and magnetic letters m a s d t i n p g o c k ck u b f e l h sh r j v y w th z ch qu x ng nk.
Put the Speed Sound cards th, i, ng in your pocket chart close together.
Point to each card as you say the sounds.
Say the word, sweeping your pointer from left to right under the word.

Repeat a few times saying the sounds and then the word with the students.
Repeat with six of these words: thin thick this zap zip chin chop chat quiz quit fox box fix six sing bang thing wing.

Copy the words onto the board.
Silently make th - i - ng on the board with the Speed Sound cards. Ask partner 1s to:
make the first word with the magnetic letters;
point to the letters to partner 2;
read the sounds and then the word to partner 2.
Repeat with the other words.
Partners take turns at being the 'teacher' - making the words.
N.B. First check that at least one partner can sound-blend. Support partners who have difficulty.

Find Green Word cards 1.6.
Point to the sounds as they read the words in Sound Talk.
Display the word in a pocket chart and return to practise.

Step 3: Sound Fingers to spell

Say: Show me three fingers.
Say the word: thing.
Model how you touch each finger firmly as you say the sounds: th-i-ng.
Model writing the word on the board.

Say the word: thing.
Ask the students to press the sounds on their fingers.
Ask the students to write the word.
Ask them to say the word in sounds as they write.
Repeat with a few words.

Blending Lesson 6 should be followed by Blending Lesson 7 to practise all Set 1 sounds.

Blending Lesson 7

For practice of blending all Set 1 sounds.

> it is vital that you avoid saying 'uh' at the end of each sound - KEEP THE SOUNDS PURE!

Step 1: Speed read the sounds

Practise reading m, a, s, d, t, i, n, p, g, o, c, k, ck, u, b, f, e, l, h, sh, r, j, v, y, w, th, z, ch, qu, x, ng, nk in and out of order at speed.

Step 2: Sound Talk to read

Give partners one magnetic board and magnetic letters m a s d t i n p g o c k ck u b f e l h sh r j v y w th z ch qu x ng nk.
Put the Speed Sound cards b, l, o, b in your pocket chart close together.
Point to each card as you say the sounds.
Say the word, sweeping your pointer from left to right under the word.

Repeat a few times saying the sounds and then the word with the students.
Repeat with six of these words: blip brat drop drip clip from frog flag flop grin gran pram prop slip slid skip trip best test bell well mess dress thing think wink.

Copy the words onto the board.
Silently make b - l - o - b on the board with the Speed Sound cards. Ask partner 1s to:
make the first word with the magnetic letters;
point to the letters to partner 2;
read the sounds and then the word to partner 2.
Repeat with the other words.
Partners take turns at being the 'teacher' - making the words.
N.B. First check that at least one partner can sound-blend. Support partners who have difficulty.

Find Green Word cards 1.7.
Point to the sounds as they read the words in Sound Talk.
Say the word with exaggerated pronunciation.
Blend b into l-o-b. Avoid bulob.
Repeat with the students.
Display the word in a pocket chart and return to practise.

Step 3: Sound Fingers to spell

Say: Show me four fingers.
Say the word: blob.
Model how you touch each finger firmly as you say the sounds: b-l-o-b.
Model writing the word on the board.

Say the word: blob.
Ask the students to press the sounds on their fingers.
Ask the students to write the word.
Ask them to say the word in sounds as they write.
Repeat with a few words.

Phonic lessons for students (continued)

The dos and don'ts of teaching Set 1 phonic lessons

Do:

- teach at least three new sounds a day
- consolidate each set of sounds before moving on
- organise short one-to-one sessions for students at risk
- keep the lessons short, active and fun (three short lessons are more effective than one long one)
- move on to the next set of five sounds when the students can read the first five - even if they still have difficulty in sound-blending
- praise their efforts constantly

Don't:

- start students on this part of the programme if they already know these sounds
- ask 'What sound can you hear at the beginning of...?' (just say the sound at the start of the word
- with them; show rather than ask)
- ask students 'Can you think of any words starting with...?'
- ask students to write letters without saying the sounds (this means that you will need to be with them when they write)
- think up lots of extra things to do (short, sharp, clear lessons are the secret of effective phonic teaching)
- ask one student to write a letter on the board (either the others get bored, or they all want a go)
- use cursive handwriting while the students are still learning to read and write (it makes it very hard for the slower learner)

Teaching students with significant learning difficulties

Students with a range of difficulties can learn the sounds, even if they are partially sighted, have poor hearing and speech production, poor concentration or poor behaviour. If a student is expected to have difficulty, a teacher or an assistant may need to be assigned to work on a one-to-one basis with him or her from the beginning. See p. 38 1-to-1 ten-minute tutoring.

Phonic lessons for students (continued)

Set 2 phonic lessons

- **Blueprint lesson plan**

This plan should be used as a blueprint for all the Set 2 phonic lessons. Follow it carefully for each new sound. You will then be able to use the summary lesson plans to teach each group of letters.

You will need:

- the Speed Sounds Cards (Set 2)
- the Green Word Cards (Set 2) displayed on a 'Green Word Wall'
- the Speed Sounds Poster

What to do:

Tell the students that they will be learning 12 new graphemes from the poster:

ay ee igh ow oo (zoo) oo (look) ar or air ir ou oy

Follow this plan for each grapheme.

Hear and say

Say 'ay' (don't show the letters). Use MTYT to sing and stretch the sound.

Introduce the phrase-picture side of the card.

Say:

This is a picture of students playing. They are saying 'may I play?'

Say each of the listed words (on the card and on page 32) in Sound Talk, e.g. 'd-ay'
Ask the students to say the whole word.

Read ay

Show the other side of the card.
Say the sound, e.g. 'ay'.
Explain that two letters are used to make the sound. Say 'two letters – one sound'.
The students repeat it after you.

Look for the grapheme on the Speed Sounds Poster.
Put the 'ay' card in your Speed Sounds pack. Practise reading the new card in a pack of Set 1 cards.

Phonic lessons for students (continued)

Set 2 phonic lessons (continued)

● Blueprint lesson plan (continued)

Speed Sounds

As each new sound is learned, the students should practise reading all the graphemes (letters/letter groups) you have taught so far from the Speed Sounds Cards.

Sound Talk for reading

Find the Green Word Cards for words containing the target grapheme:

day play may way spray

Do the following for each of these words.

Students say the word in Sound Talk.

Ask students to say the whole word.

As the students add more words to their repertoire, display the relevant Green Word Cards on the Green Word Wall.

Sound Fingers for spelling

Do the following for each of the words above.

Say the word, e.g. 'play'.
Ask the students to count the sounds. (Give them time to do this.)

Say 'fingers'.
The students raise three fingers.

Say the three sounds in Sound Talk with the students, touching a finger for each sound.

Write

Model how to write the words above, underlining 'ay'.
Ask the students to do it.

Phonic lessons for students (continued)

Set 2 phonic lessons (continued)

The dos and don'ts of teaching Set 2 phonic lessons

Do:

- teach one new sound a day and review those already taught
- show the students how to use their non-writing hand for Sound Fingers, with the palm facing them
- keep the lessons short, active and fun
- praise the students' efforts constantly

Don't:

- ask students for suggestions for words containing a particular sound
- ask students to write letters without saying the sounds (this means that you will need to be with them when they write)
- move on to the Set 3 Speed Sounds until the students can read the Set 2 sounds in and out of order, from the Speed Sounds Cards and the Speed Sounds Poster

Phonic lessons for students (continued)

Set 2 phonic lessons (continued)

- **Summary lesson plan for each sound**

ay: may I play? (day, play, may, way, say, spray)
ee: what can you see? (see, three, been, green, seen, sleep)
igh: fly high (high, night, light, fright, bright, might)
ow: blow the snow (blow, snow, low, show, know, slow)
oo: poo at the zoo (too, zoo, food, pool, moon, spoon)
oo: look at a book (took, look, book, shook, cook, foot)
ar: start the car (car, star, part, start, hard, sharp)
or: shut that door (sort, short, horse, sport, fork, snort)
air: that's not fair (fair, stair, hair, air, chair, lair)
ir: twirl and whirl (girl, bird, third, whirl, twirl, dirt)
ou: shout it out (out, shout, loud, mouth, round, found)
oy: toy for a boy (toy, boy, enjoy)

Teach the students to read the sound by:

- saying the new phrase and sound (and practising the Speed Sounds already taught)
- reading the Green Words in Sound Talk

Teach the students to write the words by:

- playing Sound Fingers
- writing the words, underlining two-letter graphemes

Phonic lessons for students (continued)

Set 3 phonic lessons

● Blueprint lesson plan

This plan should be used as a blueprint for all the Set 3 phonic lessons. Follow it carefully for each new sound. You will then be able to use the summary lesson plans to teach each group of letters.

You will need:

- the Speed Sounds Cards (Set 3)
- the Green Word Cards (Set 3) displayed on a Green Word Wall
- the Speed Sounds Poster

What to do:

Before starting this stage, teach the students the names of the letters. Letter names are now used for spelling because the students will be learning alternative graphemes for the same sound (e.g. the sound 'ee' can be written as 'ee' or 'ea').

Tell the students that they will be learning new graphemes in the sound boxes on the poster:

a-e i-e o-e u-e ea aw are ur er or ai oa ew ire ear ure (+ endings tious, cious, tion)

Follow this plan for each grapheme.

Read

Introduce the phrase-picture side of the card.

Say:

This is a picture of a student saying 'cup of tea'.

Say each of the listed words (on the card and on page 36) in Sound Talk, e.g. 'ea-t'
Ask the students to say the whole word.

Show the other side of the card.
Say the sound, e.g. 'ea'.
The students repeat after you.

Look for the grapheme on the Speed Sounds Poster.
Tell the students that they now know two graphemes with which to write this sound: 'ee' and 'ea'.
Show both Speed Sound cards together.

Phonic lessons for students (continued)

Set 3 phonic lessons (continued)

- **Blueprint lesson plan** (continued)

Speed Sounds

As each new sound is learned, the students should practise reading all the graphemes (letters/letter group) you have taught so far from the Speed Sounds Cards. Use the cards and the poster and repeat this frequently throughout the day.

Sound Talk for reading

Find the Green Word Cards for words containing the target grapheme:

tea eat neat real clean please

Do the following for each of these words.

Students say the word in Sound Talk.

Ask the students to say the whole word.

As the students add more words to their repertoire, display the relevant Green Word Cards on the Green Word Wall so you can revisit the words throughout the day.

Revise Green Words containing graphemes you have already taught.

Sound Fingers for spelling

Do the following for each of the words above.

Say the word, e.g. 'neat'.
Ask the students to count the sounds. (Give them time to do this.)

Say 'fingers'.
The students raise three fingers.

Say the three sounds in Sound Talk with the students, touching a finger for each sound.

Now give the spelling for each sound, tracing the grapheme onto a finger.

Phonic lessons for students (continued)

Set 3 phonic lessons (continued)

- **Blueprint lesson plan** (continued)

Write

Write the words on the board, underlining 'ea'.
Read each word in Sound Talk.
Say the graphemes in letter names. Say the 'ea' letter names quickly as one unit.
Rub out the words, then say the words one by one.
Ask the students to write the words.

Whenever you ask the students to spell a word containing the 'ee' sound, you will need to ask them whether to spell the word with 'ee' or 'ea'.

The dos and don'ts of teaching Set 3 phonic lessons

Do:

- teach one new sound a day and review those already taught
- show the students how to use their non-writing hand for Sound Fingers, with the palm facing them
- show them how to trace each grapheme onto the appropriate finger (persevere with this)
- draw a big hand on a piece of paper if a student has poor motor control
- keep the lessons short, active and fun
- praise the students' efforts constantly

Don't:

- use letter names for reading – only for spelling
- ask students for suggestions for words containing a particular grapheme
- hold students back who can read the graphemes and words, but have difficulty spelling

Phonic lessons for students (continued)

Set 3 phonic lessons (continued)

- **Summary lesson plan for each sound**

oi: spoil the boy (join, voice, coin)
ea: cup of tea (dream, seat, scream, real, clean, please)
e: (he, me, we, she, be)
a-e: make a cake (make, cake, name, same, late, date)
i-e: nice smile (smile, white, nice, like, time, hide)
o-e: phone home (home, hope, spoke, note, broke, phone)
u-e: huge brute (tune, rude, huge, brute, use, June)
aw: yawn at dawn (saw, law, dawn, crawl, paw, yawn)
are: share and care (care, share, dare, scare, square, bare)
ur: nurse with a purse (burn, turn, spurt, nurse, purse, hurt)
er: a better letter (never, better, weather, after, proper, corner)
ow: brown cow (how, down, brown, cow, town, now)
ai: snail in the rain (paid, snail, tail, train, paint, rain)
oa: goat in a boat (goat, road, boat, throat, toast, coat)
ew: chew the stew (chew, new, blew, flew, drew, grew)
ire: fire, fire! (fire, hire, wire, bonfire, inspire, conspire)
ear: hear with your ear (hear, dear, fear, near, year, ear)
ure: sure it's pure? (pure, sure, cure, pic`ture, mix`ture, crea`ture fu`ture, ad`ven`ture, temp`er`a`ture)

Teach the following three word endings (-tion, -cious, -tious) before the students read the last three *Modules*. Say each word in syllables - as it looks, and then as it sounds.

tion: (con`ver`sa`tion, cel`e`bra`tion, ex`plor`a`tion, trad`i`tion, con`grat`u`la`tion, a`tten`tion)
cious, tious: (de`li`cious, pre`cious, sus`pi`cious, fe`ro`cious, vi`cious, scrump`tious)

Teach the students to read the sound by:

- saying the new phrase and sound (and practising the Speed Sounds already taught)
- reading the Green Words in Sound Talk

Teach the students to write by:

- playing Sound Fingers
- writing words containing the same sound with alternative graphemes, e.g. 'ee' and 'ea'

Phonic lessons for students (continued)

Set 3 phonic lessons (continued)

• Summary lesson plan for each sound (continued)

Teaching 'a-e', 'i-e', 'o-e' and 'u-e'

These are called 'split graphemes'.

Take the 'a-e' card as an example. Explain that the 'a' and the 'e' have been split up but an arc joins them together.

Say the sound (ay), say the grapheme: a split e.
Show the picture side. Say: This child is saying 'make a cake'.
Say each of the words listed on the card in Sound Talk and ask the students to say the whole word: e.g. you say m - ay - k; the students say make.
Point to a-e on the Speed Sounds Poster. Say the sound (ay), say the grapheme: a split e.

Sound Talk for reading

Using the a-e Green Word Cards:
Point to the sounds as you read the word in Sound Talk. (Touch the a-e at the same time as you say the sound.)
Ask students to repeat in Sound Talk.
Ask students to say the whole word.

Sound Fingers for spelling

For each of the words listed on the a-e card:
Say the word, e.g. make.
Say 'fingers'. The students show three fingers.
Say the three sounds in Sound Talk with the students, touching a finger for each sound.
Trace the graphemes onto three fingers as you say the letter names
(e does not have its own finger).
Say the word again.

1-to-1 ten-minute tutoring

Which students should be tutored?

There are a few students who, for whatever reason, take longer to catch up with their reading. It is crucial to give these students extra help.

Compile a 'hotlist' of students who are making the slowest progress in learning sounds and/or sound-blending.

Work through each of the steps in the three tutoring plans below until students are confident.

Who should do the tutoring?

It is important that the students on the 'hotlist' are taught by somebody who has patience, energy, relentlessness and a real passion for teaching reading. There are many tutors who have rescued even the most 'lost' students because they have committed themselves to each student so whole-heartedly.

How many times a week and for how long should the 1-to-1 tutoring sessions be?

Each day the students should work in their homogenous group in the morning and then receive ten minutes of extra teaching in the afternoon, following exactly the same part of the programme that they were doing that morning.

The three ten-minute tutoring priorities

Priority 1: Read Speed Sounds Set 1

Start with cards m a s d t and then add a new card each day

Step 1

Show the first five cards, *picture* side up.
Ask the student to point as you say the picture card words: mountains, apple, snake, dinosaur, tower.
The student says the picture card words in and out of order at speed.

Step 2

Show the first five cards, *picture* side up.
The student stretches/bounces the first sound of the picture (information on the Speed Sounds Set 1 card): mmmmountains, a-a-a-apple, ssssnake, d-d-d-dinosaur, t-t-t-tower.
The student repeats with the cards in any order.

Step 3

Show the first five cards, *picture* side up.
The student stretches/bounces the first sound of the word and then whispers the full word: mmmmountains, a-a-a-apple, sssnake, d-d-d-dinosaur, t-t-t-tower.
The student repeats with the cards in any order.

Step 4

Show the first five cards, *picture* side up.
The student stretches/bounces the first sound of the word only: mmm, a-a-a, sss, d-d-d, t-t-t.
The student repeats with the cards in any order.

Step 5
Show the first five cards, *letter* side up.
The student stretches/bounces the sound: mmm, a-a-a, sss, d-d-d, t-t-t.
The student repeats with the cards in any order.

Step 6
Show the first five cards, *letter* side up.
The student says the short sound with no stretching or bouncing: m a s d t.
The student repeats with the cards in any order.

Step 7
Show the first five cards, *letter* side up.
The student says the short sound at speed: m a s d t.
The student repeats with the cards in any order.

Priority 2: Read by sound-blending

Step 1
Some students find sound-blending very difficult, but every student can learn to do this with perseverance.

Without the cards, say the words below in Sound Talk and then say each word.
The student should be in a position where he can see your mouth clearly.
Say the words in exaggerated Sound Talk.
Ask the student to copy your mouth movements saying every word in Sound Talk followed by an exaggerated pronunciation of the word.
Repeat with each word until the student can copy the word in Sound Talk followed by the whole word, e.g. m-a-t mat, s-a-t sat, a-t at, S-a-m Sam, a-m am, m-a-d mad.

Step 2
Start with cards m, a, s, d, t and once they can read these at speed, add a new card each day.
Use the Speed Sound Cards or the Magnetic Sounds Cards.

Place the cards on the table.
Check the student can read the sounds in and out of order and at speed.
Silently point to m, a and t.
Ask the student to make the word.
Ask the student to read the word in Sound Talk and say the word.

Pull the cards apart and say the word in Sound Talk.
Push the cards together and say the word.

Make the words sat, at, Sam, am, mad, in the same way.
Keep repeating the activity until the student can do this at speed.
Practise reading the words without Sound Talk.

Add a new sound each day to make new words.

Priority 3: Support the oldest students at the lowest levels of reading

Once all students on the programme have achieved Priority 1 and 2, select the oldest students who are reading at the lowest levels for 1-to-1 ten-minute tutoring. Reinforce whatever they are being taught in their literacy groups.

The Modules		Speed Sounds included
Introductory Module		**Speed Sounds Set 1** *Emphasis sounds:* a e i o u
		Speed Sounds Set 1 *Emphasis sounds:*
Module 1	The Thing from the Black Planet	a e i o u + cc, cvcc and ccvcc words
Module 2	A wolf cub	a e i o u + cc, cvcc and ccvcc words
Module 3	Big Malc	a e i o u + cc, cvcc and ccvcc words
		Speed Sounds Sets 1 and 2 *Emphasis sounds:*
Module 4	Hay into gold	ay
Module 5	Keeping a cat	ee
Module 6	Bill Bright's fishing trip	igh
Module 7	The yellow light	ow
Module 8	Baboons on the loose	oo
Module 9	Bart the champ	ar
Module 10	Lorna	or oor ore
Module 11	A bad hair day	air
Module 12	A good win for the red shirts	ir
Module 13	A player to be proud of	ou
		Speed Sounds Sets 1, 2 and 3 *Emphasis sounds:*
Module 14	Cook — and enjoy!	oy oi
Module 15	Late	ay a-e
Module 16	The weaving contest	ee ea
Module 17	Celia Smith's quick goldfish pie	i-e ie
Module 18	Beep!	ow o-e
Module 19	Spellbound: The tale of a lost duke	oo u-e ue
Module 20	The Outlaws	or aw au
		Speed Sounds Sets 1, 2 and 3 *Emphasis sounds:*
Module 21	Romeo and Juliet	air are
Module 22	Sunburst Teen Magazine	ir ur er
Module 23	How does it feel to be an astronaut?	ou ow
Module 24	Raiders of the lost shark	ai aigh eigh
Module 25	Jason's quest	ow o-e oa
Module 26	New boy	oo u-e ue ew
Module 27	Kevin the killer hamster	er
Module 28	Il Bello	-le -il -el -al
Module 29	Emergency	-ent -ence -ant -ance
Module 30	Creature	-ture -ure -our -or
Module 31	Macbeth	-ous -ious -cous -cious -tious
Module 32	The invisible city	-able -ably -ible -ibly
Module 33	Penalty for piracy: Execution	-tion -sion -ssion

Approximate NC level for reading if decoding well and understanding texts	Scotland: Curriculum for Excellence	Northern Ireland Curriculum	Modules	Speed Sounds known effortlessly, and blending
1c–1b	Early	Level 1	Introductory Module	Set 1 m a s d t i n p g o c k u b f e l h sh r j v y w th z ch qu x ng nk
1b–1a	Early	Level 1	1-3	Set 1 m a s d t i n p g o c k u b f e l h sh r j v y w th z ch qu x ng nk
1a–2b	Early	Level 1/2	4–13	Set 1 m a s d t i n p g o c k u b f e l h sh r j v y w th z ch qu x ng nk Set 2 ay ee igh ow oo *oo* ar or or oor ore air ir ou
2b–3b	Early/First	Level 2/3	14–20	Set 1 m a s d t i n p g o c k u b f e l h sh r j v y w th z ch qu x ng nk Set 2 ay ee igh ow oo *oo* ar or or oor ore air ir ou and from Set 3 oi a-e ea i-e ie o-e u-e ue aw au
3b–4c/b	First/Second	Level 3/4	21–33	Sets 1, 2 + 3 oi a-e ea i-e ie o-e u-e ue aw au are ur er ow ai aigh eigh o-e oa u-e ue ew plus endings: -le -il -al -ent -ence – ant -ance -ture -ure -our -or -ous -ious -cious -tious -able -ably -ible -ibly -tion -sion -ssion

There are nine reading activities.
The students:

1 Practise reading the Speed Sounds
2 Read the Green, Red and Challenge Words for the story
3 Listen to the introduction
4 Discuss the vocabulary check with you
5 Read the story
6 Re-read the story and discuss the 'questions to talk about'
7 Read the story with fluency and expression
8 Answer the 'questions to read and answer'
9 Practise reading the speed words

There are nine writing activities.
The students:

1 Play 'sound-grapheme rhythms'
2 Play 'sound-grapheme fingers'
3 Carry out a spelling check
4 Take a spelling test
5 Hold a sentence
6 Build a sentence
7 Edit for spelling/punctuation/grammar
8 Write a composition with the support of a picture strip (*Modules 1-13* only)
9 Write a guided composition with the support of a writing frame (*Modules 14-33* only)

See timetables on pages 77-80.

• Blueprint lesson plan

This plan should be used as a blueprint for all the *Module* lessons. Follow it carefully. The *Modules* should be read in order. Each *Module* contains teacher's notes which show you how to apply the plan to that particular story. All the instructions in italics should be read out by the teacher.

You will need:

- a flip chart on which to write words from the *Module*
- a Red Word Wall (for displaying the red words learned so far)
- a Vocabulary Wall
- the Speed Sounds Poster

The students will need:

- a *Module* (one each)

● Blueprint lesson plan (continued)

The nine reading activities

Activity 1: Practise reading the Speed Sounds

Purpose: to read aloud the graphemes already taught, at speed.

From the Speed Sounds Poster, read chorally the graphemes already taught. Point to the graphemes as the students pronounce the sounds clearly, in and out of order. (A few consonant graphemes, e.g. 'ss', 'll', 'ff', 'ck', are circled in the *Modules* to remind you to emphasise these.)

Next, the students work with partners to take turns in reading the Speed Sounds on page 2 of the *Module*. Tell all the sets to get into their 'perfect partner positions'.

Say 'Go.' Partner 1 keeps reading until you raise your hand.
The partners then reverse roles.
Make this session short and sharp - maximum 5 minutes.

Activity 2: Read the Green, Red and Challenge Words for the story

Purpose: to read aloud the words that will be used in the new story.

Write the Green Words (and, in later books, the Challenge Words). Underline any two-letter or three-letter graphemes on the flip chart. Display the Red Word Cards on your Red Word Wall. These are listed on page 3 of the *Module* and on each page of the *Introductory Module*.

The Green Words

Green Words with one syllable
Model how to read each word, first in fast Sound Talk and then as a complete word.
Read the words with the students, pointing to each grapheme as you say its sound.

Green Words with two or three syllables
Read each syllable, first in fast Sound Talk and then as a complete syllable:

g-ar gar d-e-n den

Read the whole word in separate syllables:

gar/den

Read the whole word.

Blueprint lesson plan (continued)

The Green Words (continued)

Green Words with endings, e.g. 'ed', 'ing'
Say the root part of the word in Sound Talk. Then read the whole word, exaggerating the ending:

groan groand (groaned)
jump jumpt (jumped)
land landid (landed)
shine shinee (shiny)

Root words ending in e, e.g. smile
When 'ed' is added, e doubles as both the ending and the grapheme i-e.

smiled

When 'ing' is added, say 'you can't have E with ING'.

Do not use Sound Talk to read the word ending.

The Red Words

These are words that need to be learned 'by sight'.
Read the Red Words introduced to date.

Say each word in fast Sound Talk, including the tricky grapheme, then say the word:

s-e-d (said)
h-oo (who)
w-o-ch (watch)

Display these words on the Red Word Wall.

The Challenge Words

These are content words which are necessary to the story.
They cannot be counted as 'Green' because they include a 'grotty grapheme', but neither can they be counted as 'Red' because they are uncommon.

Challenge the students to read the words, but help immediately if they are too challenging!

Blueprint lesson plan (continued)

Word reading in partners
In this activity, the students can practise reading the words and you can assess their decoding ability.

Tell all the sets of partners to get into their 'partner positions'. Partner 1 positions the word chart (in the *Module*) so both partners can see it. Partner 2 then points to the first word and Partner 1 gets ready to read.

Say 'Go'. Partner 1 keeps reading until you raise your hand.

The partners then reverse roles.

When the students can read these words, encourage them to read at a faster pace.

Remember to praise the students for their teaching.

Activity 3: Listen to the introduction

Purpose: to introduce the story and to motivate students to read it.

First, ask the question that will connect the story to the students' own experiences. (This is under *Introduction* on page 4 in the *Module*.)

When the students read the story for the first time, they will be decoding rather than comprehending the text, so a lively introduction is vital. The more effort you put into this introduction, the more the students will want to read the story. Always stop on a cliffhanger, so that they will want to read to the end to find out what happens.

Activity 4: Discuss the vocabulary check with you

Purpose: to explain the meanings of any unfamiliar words in the story.

Write the words (potential problem words are listed and defined under vocabulary check on page 3 in the *Module*) on the board. Read the book (before the lesson) to check that there are no other unfamiliar words or phrases.

Ask the students to read each word, using 'my turn, your turn', and then give the definition. (Avoid asking the students to suggest the meanings on the first reading. You have predicted that they will not know them!) You may want to combine Activities 3 and 4 so the students can use the vocabulary to help them predict what will happen in the story.

Blueprint lesson plan (continued)

Activity 5: Read the story

Purpose: for partners to read the text independently.

The students are now ready to read the text for themselves; they have practised reading the graphemes and words, you have explained any new vocabulary, and you have motivated them to want to read the story.

Give each pair two copies of the *Module* (but place one on top of the other while each student is reading). Ask them to turn to the story or passage. Partner 1 (the teacher) listens attentively as Partner 2 reads one page of the book. Teach the students what to do if their partner cannot read a word. When the reader hesitates, the teaching partner should:

- pause and count to three in his or her head
- prompt – encourage his or her partner to use Sound Talk
- praise when his or her partner is successful

The partners then reverse roles so that Partner 2 is reading the next page of the book.

The students read to the end of the story. Early finishers go back to the beginning. (This may mean that some partnerships read the story twice in the same time as others take to read it once.)

This is an important time for you to assess the students' progress. Do not sit with one partnership.

Praise the students for their good teaching.

By *Module 10,* allow one partner to point to his or her own book as he or she reads. The other partner points in his or her own book. You can then easily check how well the teaching partner is following.

When the students have read the book once, use 'jump in'. Each student has a copy of the *Module.* Read the text to them slowly, hesitating on particular words so that the students can 'jump in'. As you read, check that all the students are tracking word-by-word. 'Think aloud' at the end of each page, summarising what has happened.

Blueprint lesson plan (continued)

Activity 6: Re-read the story and discuss the 'questions to talk about'

Purpose: to gain greater understanding of the text; to find answers to questions by locating information in the text; to give reasons for answers.

These questions, in italics, are on page 7 of the *Module*. The teacher should read them out.

The students re-read the whole book. Then ask students to turn to their partners to discuss the main idea(s) in each section before moving on to discuss the 'questions to talk about'.

Read one of the 'questions to talk about' to the students.

Tell them whether it is a 'find it' question or a 'prove it' question.

('Find it' questions require the students to find a literal answer in the text. Make sure all the students locate the information in the text, even if they know the answer from memory. 'Prove it' questions require the students to provide evidence and/or to give reasons for their answers. These questions require students to infer meaning from the text.)

Ask the partners to decide on their answers, and then choose one or two students to report back to the group. Do not ask the students to write down their answers.

Praise the students for their good partner work.

Blueprint lesson plan (continued)

Reading to develop fluency, expression and comprehension

Activity 7: Read the story with fluency and expression

Purpose: to increase students' understanding of the text by considering how to use appropriate intonation and expression.

When the students can use appropriate voices to show the mood of the passage and the emotions of the characters, they are reading with greater understanding.

Think aloud about how you would read a page. Ask yourself questions, as though you are talking to yourself. Model how you use words and phrases to describe the characters' feelings, e.g. angry, furious, sad, tired, jealous, irritable, grumpy, surprised, full of anticipation, anxious, desperate, in despair.

e.g. *Module* 6. How does Bill feel when he gets to his hotel room and opens his case?

Choose a few sections that will be interesting to discuss. Ask students to read a line or paragraph and then discuss how they think a character is feeling. Encourage students to justify their reasons for deciding how a character feels or behaves.

Choose a few partners to report back each time.

Model how to read expressively with a partner after discussing the mood of the text and the characters' feelings.

Ask partners to practise reading selected passages.

Build up, cumulatively, a display of words that describe characters' feelings and emotions.

When a student reads with expression, they are attending to many things at once:

they decode effortlessly and automatically

they connect previous knowledge and events in their life to what they read

they predict what is about to come in the next part of the story

their eyes scan ahead of what they are saying

they build mind-pictures as they read

they re-read when something does not make sense

they empathise with the characters

most importantly, they are making connections and integrating ideas between one passage and the next

When a student reads with appropriate intonation and expression we know, in the main, that they are understanding what they read.

Most of us have asked a student who is reading in a monotone to 'put more expression' in their voice. However, what we are actually asking the child to do is all of the above at the same time.

Merely showing the students how we read aloud goes only a little way to help them read with appropriate intonation.

We use three ways to help students read with a greater understanding:

- thinking about how the character feels
- deciding keywords
- building mind pictures

Use one or two of these for each text.

Activity 8: Answer the 'questions to read and answer'

Purpose: for students to answer questions independently and to record their answers quickly.

The questions to read and answer are on page 7 of the *Module*. They are written in words that the students can decode. They require the students to circle the correct answer, complete a sentence or write a full answer.

Model how to work out the answers by searching back in the text.

Partners should check that they have the same answers (when they have both recorded their answers independently).

Activity 9: Practise reading the Speed Words

Purpose: To assess whether students can read the words effortlessly without using Sound Talk or the context of the story as a support.

Once the students can read the text effortlessly, they should practise reading the speed words on page 11 of the *Module* as quickly as possible. They should read across the rows and down the columns, and then in and out of order. Partners take it in turns to do this, continuing until they can read the whole page effortlessly. If a student hesitates or makes an error, he or she starts again at the beginning of the row or column.

Monitor students' progress as they practise reading.

Fresh Start Anthologies

For every *Fresh Start Module* there are accompanying texts in the *Fresh Start Anthologies* and *More Anthologies* to encourage wider reading. These can be used for library time, home reading or further practice of the sounds and graphemes focused on in the *Fresh Start Modules*. They contain a variety of lively non-fiction, poetry and fiction texts, including quizzes, playscripts, and comic strips to motivate students to read for pleasure.

The *Anthologies* and *More Anthologies* texts should be read after each *Module* is completed, to ensure students are reading within their phonic knowledge and experience success in reading.

Each *Module* has a linked text in both the *Anthologies* and *More Anthologies*. They provide practice of the same graphemes, so either can be read first. For example, Text 4 in the *Anthologies* provides practice of the 'ay' sound as focused on in *Module 4*, and Text 4 in the *More Anthologies* provides further practice of the 'ay' sound. See the chart on pp. 40–41 showing the sounds practised.

Because the subjects of the *Anthologies* and *More Anthologies* texts are linked to the *Modules*, some of the vocabulary students meet will be familiar, which supports independent reading.

Module	Linked Anthologies text	Linked More Anthologies text
1 The Thing from the Black Planet	1 A penpal from the Black Planet	1 Planets 'R' Us Travel
2 A wolf cub	2 Challenge Prof. the Boff!	2 Fang hunts with the pack
3 Big Malc	3 Hank Stock – strong man	3 Tests of strength
4 Hay into gold	4 Six top tricks!	4 Inca bling!
5 Keeping a cat	5 The day of the dog	5 Calling all dogs – the police need you!

Module	Linked Anthologies text	Linked More Anthologies text
6 Bill Bright's fishing trip	6 High heels – or string vests?	6 Fish with Fred
7 The yellow light	7 Know your fright limit!	7 Camping? Forget it!
8 Baboons on the loose	8 Do you do zoos?	8 Top bananas
9 Bart the champ	9 Fast track facts	9 Speed, skids and mud!
10 Lorna	10 Stay cool in school!	10 Which school is for you?

Module	Linked Anthologies text	Linked More Anthologies text
11 A bad hair day	11 Lairy hair	11 Mrs Fairborn's baby
12 A good win for the red shirts	12 What sort of football fan are you?	12 It's football – but not as we know it!
13 A player to be proud of	13 Norman Knight, time-travelling superstar	13 Christmas 1914
14 Cook – and enjoy!	14 Troy Tomato cooks up a storm	14 Unwrap – and enjoy!
15 Late	15 Room rage	15 Get your skates on!

Module	Linked Anthologies text	Linked More Anthologies text
16 The weaving contest	16 Peacocks or peanuts – Dr Dean looks at strange phobias	16 Monsters of land, air and sea
17 Celia Smith's quick goldfish pie	17 Down the hatch!	17 Wild Mike's guide to staying alive!
18 Beep!	18 The phone zone	18 Home grown sound effect zone!
19 Spellbound	19 Duke weds royal bride in wedding of the season!	19 Happy ever after?
20 The Outlaws	20 Awesome!	20 The Fab Factor

Module	Linked Anthologies text	Linked More Anthologies text
21 Romeo and Juliet	21 A fanfare for Monio and Oojilet	21 Once upon a love match
22 Sunburst Teen Magazine	22 Ask Shirley	22 Many happy returns Sunburst!
23 How does it feel to be an astronaut?	23 A spell in space	23 They came from outer space!
24 Raiders of the lost shark	24 Do it!	24 Shark for sale
25 Jason's quest	25 Left alone to die - the story of Alexander Selkirk	25 Extreme survival

Module	Linked Anthologies text	Linked More Anthologies text
26 New boy	26 Keep fit for footy	26 New school blues
27 Kevin the killer hamster	27 The flight of Freddy Fish	27 The dog ate my homework!
28 Il Bello	28 Life on a cattle ranch	28 Watch that turtle hurtle!
29 Emergency	29 Odd achievements	29 Emergency – the A and E department
30 Creature	30 Creature features	30 Monster

Module	Linked Anthologies text	Linked More Anthologies text
31 Macbeth	31 Superstitions – sense or nonsense?	31 A famous writer – Shakespeare
32 The invisible city	32 23rd August AD 79 – a terrible day	32 Mission impossible!
33 Penalty for piracy: Execution	33 Ballad of a pirate of distinction	33 Pirate application pack
	Grand theft at Bagshot Manor – an extended read	Survivors – an extended read

● Blueprint lesson plan (continued)

The nine writing activities

Activity 1: Play 'sound-grapheme rhythms'

Purpose: for students to identify sounds and graphemes in the given words (see the spelling lists in the *Module*).

Ask the students to turn to the spelling section on page 10 of their *Module*.

Green Words

Students:
Draw a dot under each one-letter grapheme.

Draw a line under each two- or three-letter grapheme.

Draw an arc to join each split grapheme (a-e, i-e, o-e, u-e).

Complete the charts individually and then check with their partner to see is they have the same answers.

Check the answers together as a group.

Red Words

Complete as above and circle the grotty grapheme.

Ask students which grapheme they would expect to see.

Your words

Identify common errors in students' writing. Ask them to copy these words from the board into the space provided in their books.

Analyse the words as above.

● Blueprint lesson plan (continued)

Activity 2: Play 'sound-grapheme fingers'

Purpose: for students to remember the spelling of a word (just for single syllabic and Red Words).

The Green Words and Red or Challenge Words are on page 10 of the *Module*.
The students' *Modules* should be shut now.

<u>Say one of the Green Words:</u> train

The students count the sounds on their fingers (silently).

Say 'fingers'.

The students raise four fingers.

Check all the fingers (making a mental note to help any student who has a different number) and then raise your own four fingers.

Say the four sounds with the students, everyone touching a finger for each sound.

Say 'graphemes'.

The students should place their hands flat and 'trace-write' each of the four graphemes on a finger, saying the letter names. Repeat with the other Green Words.

<u>Say one of the Red Words:</u> there

The students count the sounds on their fingers (silently).

Say 'fingers'.

The students raise two fingers. Check all the fingers (making a mental note to help any student who has a different number) and then raise your own two fingers.

Say the two sounds with the students, everyone touching a finger for each sound.

Say 'graphemes'.

The students should place their hands flat and 'trace-write' each of the two graphemes on a finger, saying the letter names once they are learning Speed Sounds Set 3. Repeat with the other Red Words.

- **Blueprint lesson plan** (continued)

Ask the students to name the 'grotty grapheme': ere.

Check that:

- students raise their non-writing hand in the air
- they raise their hands with their palms facing them
- they 'write' the graphemes with the index finger of their writing hand, in the correct reading direction, and with the palm facing up!

Note: there is a space in the *Module* on page 10 *Your Words* for students' common errors to be added.

Activity 3: Carry out a spelling check

Purpose: for students to check their partner's spelling.

Each set of partners decides on the two words on the spelling list on page 10 of the *Module* that they think are the hardest to spell. They must also decide on the 'surprising' grapheme in each word. They write the two words with these graphemes highlighted.

Collect the words and write them on the board.

Say the sounds as you write each word: h-or-se.

Say the letter names as you underline each grapheme: h or se.

Ask the students to name the surprising grapheme: se.

Look for it on the Complex Speed Sounds Poster (if it's a Green Word).

The students then work in pairs to help each other to learn to spell the words, five at a time.

Model how they should test each other:
Partner 1 says a word from the list and Partner 2 writes the word.
Partner 1 checks the word and asks Partner 2 to rewrite any grapheme that has been incorrectly spelled.
The partners then reverse roles.

- **Blueprint lesson plan** (continued)

Activity 4: Take a spelling test

Purpose: for students to check their knowledge of spelling.

The students should enjoy this test: it should be a celebration of what they can do rather than a demonstration of what they cannot. Make the test formal but fun.

Say each word from the spelling list on page 10 of the *Module*.
The students write it down in their exercise books.

At the end of the test, mark the work together by saying each word in graphemes, using letter names. The students correct any incorrect graphemes with a coloured pen. (Ask them to 'share an error' as you mark, so you can all revise the spelling of a word together.)

Activity 5: Hold a sentence

Purpose: to spell words containing the graphemes taught to date; to remember and write a whole sentence at a time (these sentences are provided on pages 59-61 of this handbook or on page 26 of the *Introductory Module*).

Say one of the sentences to the whole group. Ask all the students to repeat it.
In the early stages, it may help some students if you model writing the sentences first.

Say each word of the sentence, identifying the individual sounds in Sound Talk and ticking them off on your fingers. Say the whole word, and then write it down. Re-read the completed sentence, asking the students to help you to remember each word. (Don't ask a student to do any of the writing – it takes too long and they can't all have a go.)

Rub out the sentence, and ask the students to walk to their tables. When they are all seated, holding their (sharp!) pencils in the air and with their *Modules* open at Hold a sentence, say the sentence again, miming writing a huge capital letter to start the sentence and thumping the air to mark the full stop. The students must be able to memorise the whole sentence before starting to write.

Say 'Go'. The students should write as quickly as possible. Observe their writing. If a student misses out a grapheme, you may wish to pop in an insertion mark - or you may decide to be pleased with whatever he or she has written! Make a note of anything you need to stress the next time you model 'holding a sentence'.

You should find it unnecessary to model writing the sentence after *Module 5*.

In the later books where there are two or three sentences, ask students to 'hold' one at a time.

● Blueprint lesson plan (continued)

Activity 6: Build a sentence

Purpose: to build a sentence around a 'vocabulary' word from the *Module.*

Display the chosen word from the vocabulary list (see page 10 of the *Module*).
Ask students to turn to their partners to give the meaning of this word.
Ask students to turn to their partners to discuss different settings/characters/situations where you might use this word.

Model, out loud, how to take some of the ideas and develop them into sentences. (Do not write yet.)
Check that the chosen word is in the sentence.

Draft one of these ideas into a sentence. Model how to extend and develop ideas on the board, crossing out and inserting words as you go (no rubber!).

Ask students to construct their own sentence with their partner - encourage students to choose a different setting and situation to yours.

When you are happy that the students know what they will write, ask them to draft their own sentence, using the chosen word.
Read out good examples as the students write.
Choose one example and model how to redraft it further with the class.

Activity 7: Edit for spelling/punctuation/grammar

Edit 1
Purpose: to search for common spelling or punctuation errors.
Write the sentence, with the errors, onto the board (see page 10 of the *Module*).
Tell the students how many errors they must find in the passage provided in the *Module.*

Search
The students read the text individually and search for the errors.

Check
The partners check that they have found the same errors. If not, they must decide who is right.

Report
Choose students to report back the errors they found, and write these on the board. Support students with any errors they have missed.

Edit 2
Purpose: to develop vocabulary.

Ask students to turn to page 11 of the *Module.* Students complete the activity individually and then check their answers with their partners, so changes can be made before you discuss these with the group.

● Blueprint lesson plan (continued)

Activity 8: Write a composition based on a picture strip (*Modules 1-13* only)

Purpose: for students to retell the story using their grapheme knowledge to date; to encourage students to write their ideas down quickly.

The picture story strip on page 9 of the *Module* provides students with a 'scaffold' for writing so that their ideas can flow easily. When students can write with confidence, it is more likely that they will enjoy writing. The story they will write is based on the story they have read, but this must be developed in any way the students choose. It is not a sequencing activity, so there is no cutting out, pasting or colouring! The aim is for students to write.

Ask the students to look at the first picture and think of a sentence that could be used to start the story.

Partner 1 tells his or her idea to Partner 2.
Partner 2 thinks of something he or she can add or develop.
Check that the students know their first whole sentence before starting to write.
Ask a couple of students (that you have supported) to share their sentences with the rest of the group.

Repeat the above with the next picture, reversing the partners' roles.

You may wish to model one of the sentences to show the students how you would like them to use their phonic knowledge to spell new words. Say a whole word in Sound Talk before you write it down. Try this with one or two Red Words, too.

Encourage the students to write as much as possible about each picture. Avoid mentioning spelling (other than what is said above), handwriting or punctuation! Their heads should be full of ideas, not worries. Praise students for applying their knowledge of graphemes to attempt to spell words.

● Blueprint lesson plan (continued)

Activity 9: Writing a guided composition with the support of a writing frame (*Modules 14-33*)

Purpose: for students to begin to compose their own writing.

Deconstruction
Students read the text on page 8 of the *Module* in pairs.
Ask the questions in italics. (It is not intended that the students will be able to read these questions.)

Message questions
These are written in bold and relate to the content of the passage.

Form questions
These are written in plain text and relate to the structure and style of the passage.
Always ask students to turn to their partners to discuss every question.
Use different methods of feedback each time. (See Appendix G.)
Build vocabulary lists from this exercise so you can build on students' knowledge module-by-module.

Writing the composition
The notes in the writing frames set the scene for the students' writing. The students have to make decisions about what they would do in a given situation. The notes in the margin provide the teacher with a scaffold for the writing. These notes are not for the students to read. Develop these notes by using other relevant questions in order to motivate and enthuse the students.

Choose one or two students to report back after considering each question. Ask more questions to probe further.

Think aloud as you go, adding and building on students' responses to extend the vocabulary they are using.

Try to incorporate words from 'build a sentence' and make strong links from the deconstruction text.

- **Hold a sentence**

Module	Sentence
1	It was big and black with lots of lumps on its neck. It had ten fangs and six tusks. It crept along on bent legs.
2	He has spotted me. I run on stiff legs and slink up to some rocks. The man cannot get into this gap.
3	Then last spring Big Malc did all that stuff with the eggs. He put the eggs on a shelf in his flat. But they melted before he went back to get them.
4	Kay began to sob. But then in hopped an elf. 'I will spin the hay into gold if you pay me with that ring.'
5	You will need a cat bed, feeding dishes, a tray for the cat to wee in, a brush, things for the cat to play with such as ping pong balls.
6	He went to the shops and got a bright green bag. Back at his flat, he packed his fishing kit. He sat on the lid to shut it very tight.
7	Rowan was sick of looking at trees and sick of washing in a plastic bowl. And she was so sick of Lee Haddow. He was a show off.
8	Willow put down one fact about the food. Then she put down the pen. 'This is so uncool!' she sighed.
9	On the big day, Bart went off in his car. At the track he went to a snack bar and had a hot dog. Then he went to the starting post.
10	The next thing was I was finishing a story for an English project. Kelly grabbed it when Miss Owen was marking a book.
11	Willow picked up a cloth and started to rub at a blob of goo that was stuck on the hairbrush. 'I've been thinking,' she said to Rowan.

- **Hold a sentence** (continued)

Module	Sentence
12	The ref ducked to miss the ball, but it got him on the chin and he fell in the dirt. Feelings ran high and the fans swirled flags in the air.
13	Flat out on the ground after he was fouled, David kicks out. The ref shouts at him and sends him off! David slouches off and England must play with just ten men.
14	Tip the oil into a shallow pan. Put the pan on the gas or electric ring and swirl the oil around as the pan gets hot. Cook a test pancake to avoid disappointment.
15	My mate has a tame snake. It ate a rake and got in a rage. It bit my mate on the arm. He was in such a state.
16	I pick you up and hang you from the beam. No one will help you or hear your small voice. Start weaving for the rest of your days.
17	First catch your potato, dice it and put it in the freezer. Boil the ice cream. Mix the rice pudding with your feet. Mix in the ripe cheese.
18	Jack picked up his bike and rode home alone. He wanted a phone like all his mates. I know my mum will say no. Maybe Grandad will help.
19	First came the queen of the witches, sitting on a huge, black horse. Then came the elfin knight riding a large, white charger. He was one cool dude.
20	A burst of applause greeted The Outlaws as they ran onto the stage. There was a big audience. "Hello boys and girls!" shouted Saul. He sat down to play.
21	In the soft light of the flare, he saw a girl who was as fair as the sun, with eyes as bright as sapphires. She was quite beyond compare.
22	They lurk in wait for me. At first they just teased me about my curly hair. Now they have started kicking me and trying to take my bag.

- **Hold a sentence** (continued)

Module	Sentence
23	When the countdown is almost finished, the engines are ignited. You can feel the craft shaking now. It rises from the ground and through the cloud which surrounds the earth.
24	I am now claiming my money back. Let me make it quite plain that if you fail to return my payment I will make your life very difficult indeed.
25	When it was afloat, Jason loaded the boat with supplies and enlisted lots of sailors. The Argo left Greece and sailed through rough seas to a distant land.
26	He pretended that he couldn't chew the stew. He spat it out onto his plate. It was disgusting. He is such a creep. We just blew him out.
27	Kevin stood at the desk, puffing out his chest like a prize boxer. Miss Baker chased him with her stapler, but he was much too fast for her.
28	The local people set up tables with candles in the middle. They had laughed far into the night. There was plenty of optimism about Il Bello's chances of winning.
29	If you are present at the scene of an emergency, there are things you can do to help. Learn some important rules so you know what to do.
30	The idea filled me with horror. But I had injured this creature. I could help him to change his wicked behaviour and also put right my error.
31	She drugs his two servants and approaches the king's bed. But as she looks into his sleeping face, she thinks he looks like her father. She is unable to do the terrible deed.
32	I trotted up the rough track with my cartload of wood, sniffing the crisp air and looking around me. I could see the sea and the beautiful mountains.
33	The government of Jamaica was determined to stamp out the pirates, who were stealing valuable cargoes. The ship was attacked but Anne and Mary fought to the bitter end.

Pre-test and Entry test

Pre-test

Please use a standardised word- or sentence-reading test (not a comprehension test) before students start on this programme. Re-test the students at the end of each year, and keep this data for your information. Many schools use the Salford Test as it is quick to administer.

Entry test

It is important that the manager of the *Read Write Inc. Fresh Start* programme administers this test to all the students in order to achieve consistency of judgement. (In a large school, use two or three experienced teachers, but moderate your judgements first.)

See also page 11 for key points on grouping students.

Starting point: Modules

The passages are taken from the *Modules*. Start the student on the *Module* that matches the last text he or she read confidently, with fluency and intonation that shows understanding. They will also need to know all the Speed Sounds that are contained in the *Module*.

Remember that students' current sound/grapheme knowledge must always be well ahead of those sounds included in the text (*Module*) they are working on. They must also be able to sound-blend efficiently. If they cannot do that, then they will not be able to read the words in the text and therefore will not be able to access the meaning of the text. The blending lessons (pages 21–27) are designed to teach this skill through Sound Talk (for reading) and Sound Fingers (for spelling).

Starting point: Phonics

- Many *Fresh Start* students will only need to *practise* pure pronunciation or *review* existing knowledge of Speed Sounds Set 1 and blending. They will then be *taught* all of Speed Sounds Set 2 and then Speed Sounds Set 3 thoroughly and systematically, using the blueprint lesson plans as they work through the *Modules*.
- Other *Fresh Start* students will need to do as above, but may need to be *taught* (using the Speed Sounds Set 1 blueprint lesson plans) certain more tricky/less familiar Set 1 Speed Sounds, e.g. th, qu, ng.
- A few *Fresh Start* students will need to be taught each Set 1 Speed Sound using the blueprint lesson plans as if they had never seen them before. Some of these students may also need more time spent on sound-blending.

Starting point for all students on the programme

Explain to these students that:

- we use 44 speech sounds to speak every word in the English language, e.g. d-o-g, c-l-a-p, s-t-a-n-d
- every word we speak is made up of individual speech sounds that are spoken so quickly we hardly notice them

- when you spell any word, you are writing down these speech sounds, e.g. 'dog': d-o-g (3), 'clap': c-l-a-p (4), 'stand': s-t-a-n-d (5)

Show the Speed Sounds Chart.

- Explain that there are 44 sound boxes – one sound in each box.
- Explain that each of the 44 sounds is spelled with one or two letters. Each spelling of a sound is called a grapheme. Grapheme means 'writing' in Greek.
- Explain that each sound box shows different ways of spelling that sound (different graphemes). Give examples, e.g.
  - the sound ay is spelled 'ay' in day, 'ai' in train, a-e in make and 'eigh' in eight.
  - the sound f is spelled 'f' in fun, 'ff' in huff and 'ph' in phone.
- Explain that there are always the same number of speech sounds as graphemes in a word even though there may be more letters, e.g.
  - cat has three speech sounds: c-a-t and three graphemes: 'c' – 'a' – 't'.
  - shop has three speech sounds: sh-o-p and three graphemes: 'sh'-'o'-'p'.
  - light has three speech sounds: l-igh-t and three graphemes: 'l'-'igh'-'t'.
  - green has four speech sounds: g-r-ee-n and four graphemes: 'g'-'r'-'ee'-'n'.
- Explain that, as we have only 26 letters to write all the 44 speech sounds, letters are used in different combinations to write different sounds.
- Explain that they are going to learn how to hear, say, read and write all the 44 sounds and how to use Sound Talk for reading whole words and Sound Fingers for writing whole words.

National Curriculum reading levels

Approximate NC level for reading if decoding well and understanding texts	Scotland: Curriculum for Excellence	Northern Ireland Curriculum	Modules completed	Speed Sounds known effortlessly and blending
1c - 1b	Early	Level 1	Introductory	Set 1
1b - 1a	Early	Level 1	1 - 3	Set 1
1a - 2b	Early	Level 1/2	4 - 13	Sets 1 + 2
2b - 3b	Early/First	Level 2/3	14 - 20	Sets 1, 2 + 3 (oi, a-e, ea, i-e, ie, o-e, u-e, ue, aw, au)
3b - 4c/b	First/ Second	Level 3/4	21 - 33	Sets 1, 2 + 3 (are, ur, er, ow, ai, aigh, eigh, o-e, oa, u-e, ue, ew plus endings: -le, -il, -al, -ent, -ence, -ant, -ance, -ture, -ure, -our, -or, -ous, -ious, -cious, -tious, -able, -ably, -ible, -ibly, -tion, -sion, -ssion)

Entry test

Entry point to Read Write Inc. Fresh Start

Last passage student read with confidence (unaided)	**Starting point: Phonics** – *you will need to spend time teaching blending and all the sounds included in their first Module before they are asked to read it.*	**Starting point: Module**
No passage, few sounds	Teach all Speed Sounds Set 1 using the cards and the Simple Speed Sounds chart. Teach *blending* using Sound Talk.	**No Module** *Students need to be secure on Set 1 sounds and blending before they read any Modules.*
No passages, many sounds	Practise pure pronunciation of known Speed Sounds Set 1 and teach unknown Speed Sounds Set 1 using the cards and the Simple Speed Sounds chart. Teach *blending* using Sound Talk.	**No Module** *Students need to be secure on Set 1 sounds and blending before they read any Modules.*
Passage 1	Practise pure pronunciation of Speed Sounds Set 1 using the cards and the Simple Speed Sounds chart. Start teaching Speed Sounds Set 2 using the cards and the chart. Teach and/or practise blending.	**Introductory Module** *Students need to be secure on Set 1 sounds and blending before they read this Module.*
Passage 2	Practise pure pronunciation of Speed Sounds Set 1 using the Simple Speed Sounds chart. Teach Speed Sounds Set 2 using the cards and the chart. Teach and/or practise blending.	**Module 1** *Students need to be secure on Set 1 sounds and blending before they read this Module.*
Passage 3	Practise pure pronunciation of Speed Sounds Set 1 using the Simple or Complex Speed Sounds chart. Teach Speed Sounds Set 2 (see next column) using the cards and the chart. Teach and/or practise blending.	**Module 6** *Students need to be secure on Set 1 & Set 2* **ay**, **ee**, **igh** *Sounds and blending before they read this Module.*
Passage 4	Practise pure pronunciation of Speed Sounds Set 1 using the Complex Speed Sounds chart. Teach all of Speed Sounds Set 2 using the cards and the chart. Start teaching Speed Sounds Set 3 (see next column) using the cards and the chart. Teach and/or practise blending.	**Module 15** *Students need to be secure on Set 1, all of Set 2 and Set 3 sounds* **oi**, **a-e** *and blending before they read this Module.*
Passage 5	Practise pure pronunciation of Speed Sounds Set 1 using the Complex Speed Sounds chart. Teach all of Speed Sounds Set 2 using the cards and the chart. Teach Speed Sounds Set 3 (see next column) using the cards and the chart. Teach and/or practise blending.	**Module 21** *Students need to be secure on Set 1, all of Set 2 and Set 3 sounds* **oi**, **a-e**, **ea**, **i-e**, **ie**, **o-e**, **u-e**, **ue**, **aw**, **au**, **are** *and blending before they read this Module.*
Passage 6	It is unlikely that the student needs *Read Write Inc. Fresh Start*	

Pre-test and entry test

Sounds

m	a	s	d	t	i	n	p
g	o	c	k	u	b	f	e
l	h	sh	r	j	v	y	
w	th	z	ch	qu	x	ng	

Passage 1

Dan is off to Hill Crest Camp
with his pals Ben and Sam.
This is his list of things to
pack in his rucksack.

Entry test

Passage 2

Quick as a flash, Big Malc grabs
his Eminem DVD and runs off.
He runs to Snatch Smith's caravan.
(Snatch Smith is his best pal.)

"Look at this, Snatch," he brags.

Big Malc and Snatch look in the
DVD box.

"But it's empty!" says Big Malc.

"All the boxes in DVD shops
are empty!" says Snatch.
"The DVDs are kept in the back!"

"Why's that, then?" says Big Malc.

"So that they don't get nicked!" says Snatch.

Entry test

Passage 3

Then they went into the bathroom.

“Sit on this chair,” instructed Willow.

She started to mix up a bowl of maroon goo.

“Will you be putting that stuff on my hair?” gasped Rowan.

“It’s okay,” said Willow.
“It’s Fairy Dust, from Claire Blair. It’s just for fair hair.
It looks a bit funny in the bowl – but your hair will soon
look fantastic! You’ll see!”

“Next, I will wash your hair with lemon shampoo,”
said Willow.

She washed Rowan’s hair.
She rinsed it.
She dried it with a blast of hot air ...

Entry test

Passage 4

In the city of Verona, there were two important families: the Montagues and the Capulets.
The Montagues and the Capulets hated each other.
Romeo was a Montague, so when Lord and Lady Capulet gave a grand ball, he had to hide his face behind a mask.
He could not risk being seen by a Capulet.

When he had danced and eaten his fill, he stood by a pillar to rest. And there, in the soft light of a flare, he saw a girl who was as fair as the sun, with eyes as bright as sapphires. She was quite beyond compare!
Romeo stood and stared. He took her hand, and kissed it. He was captivated. He wanted to share his life with her. But who was she?

Entry test

Passage 5

And now Bruno and Lucca were finding seats near the side of the track.
The buildings around the square looked very festive, with decorative banners dangling from the windows and crowds of excited people crammed into every space.

First came the parade. Carnival floats from the local villages, city officials, traders, noble families, buglers and minstrels – and, best of all, a chariot pulled by two white bulls. In the chariot lay the Palio – the triumphal banner which would be presented to the winner.

Entry test

Passage 6

Anne Bonny

Anne Cormac was born in Ireland in 1697. Her parents took their young daughter to Carolina, USA, where her father had bought a plantation.

The Cormacs had plenty of money and a good position in society, and Anne was spoiled. She was a badly behaved girl with an angry expression, and is even said to have stabbed a maid to death in anger. Bored with plantation life as a teenager, she ran away to marry a pirate called Jack Bonny. Her furious father disinherited her, and in retaliation, Anne burned down his plantation.

Ongoing phonic/word knowledge assessment

Assess students' phonic knowledge, blending ability and knowledge of Red Words.

Put all the information onto the spreadsheet and track the students' progress term by term.

Name of student ________________________________ DOB ____________________

Assessment		Total Score	Score & Date	Score & Date	Score & Date	Score & Date
A: Speed Sounds Cards Set 1	known	31				
	at speed	31				
B: Oral sound-blending		20				
C: Sound-blending for reading	VC/CVC	10				
	CVC	10				
	CCVC and CVCC	10				
D: Red Words		10				
E: Speed Sounds Cards Set 2	known	12				
	at speed	12				
F: Sound-blending for reading	real words	12				
	nonsense words	12				
G: Two-syllable words		10				
H: Red Words		15				
I: Speed Sounds Cards Set 3	known	17				
	at speed	17				
J: Sound-blending for reading	real words	18				
	nonsense words	10				
K: Multi-syllabic words		12				
L: Red Words		30				
Total		***300***				

Assessment A: Speed Sounds Cards Set 1

One tick – knows the sound. Two ticks – can read at speed.

m	a	s	d	t
i	n	p	g	o
c	k	u	b	f
e	l	h	sh	r
j	v	y	w	th
z	ch	qu	x	ng
nk				

Total known	/31

At speed	/31

Assessment B: Oral sound-blending

Say the word in pure Sound Talk. Ask the student to say the word.

s-i-t	m-e-n	c-a-t	ch-i-n	c-u-p	n-e-ck	p-o-t	l-e-g	sh-o-p	p-a-n
b-a-ck	r-a-t	s-a-t	g-o-t	t-a-p	b-o-p	p-e-t	j-o-t	p-e-g	h-u-g

Total	/20

Assessment C: Sound-blending for reading Speed Sounds Set 1

Before using this assessment, check the students can read these sounds from the chart, at speed:

s t f n a m h o sh u d g o w p b i l j u e r

Ask the student to read the word in Sound Talk, then say the whole word.

on	in	am	at	it
and	him	had	mum	mad

Total	/10

mid	gap	lid	fog	pin
fig	mud	den	bug	dot

Total	/10

slip	press	flap	drop	glum
best	jump	crash	hand	stand

Total	/10

Assessment D: Red Words

Ask the student to read these words 'on sight'.

I	the	my	you	said
your	are	be	he	no

Total	/10

Assessment E: Speed Sounds Cards Set 2

One tick – knows the sound. Two ticks – can read at speed.

oy	ay	ow	igh	oo	oo
ou	or	ir	air	ar	ee

Known	/12

At speed	/12

Assessment F: Sound-blending for reading Speed Sounds Set 2

Before using this assessment, check the students can read the sounds in Assessment E at speed.

Ask the student to read the word in Sound Talk, then say the whole word.

Real words

tray	steep	slight	blow	spoon	start
snort	firm	stair	cook	toy	cloud

Total	/12

Nonsense words

fleef	glight	stoon	snoy	strow	slout
doy	clook	jair	mirn	jort	clarf

Total	/12

Assessment G: Two-syllable words

Ask the student to use sounds and syllables to read the words if they cannot read the word 'on sight'.

gremlin	dishcloth	farmyard	cartoon	lightning
shallow	snowman	songbird	cookbook	kitchen

Total	/10

Assessment H: Red Words

Ask the student to read these words 'on sight'.

what	all	no	we	so
to	me	call	her	there
want	go	old	some	he

Total	/15

Assessment I: Speed Sounds Cards Set 3

One tick – knows the sound. Two ticks – can read at speed.

a-e	ea	i-e	ai	oa	o-e
are	u-e	ur	ew	ow	oi
ire	ear	ure	er	aw	

Known	/17	At speed	/17

Assessment J: Sound-blending for reading Speed Sounds Set 3

Before using this assessment, check the student can read the sounds in Assessment I at speed.

Ask the student to read the word in Sound Talk, then say the whole word.

Real words

fame	stream	kite	paint	groan	bone
spare	flute	burn	chew	brown	choice
spire	fear	cure	letter	frown	paw

Total	/18

Nonsense words

plake	throke	cleab	rike	gure
flape	yice	fripe	sleam	thruke

Total	/10

Assessment K: Multi-syllabic words

Ask the student to use sounds and syllables to read the words if they cannot read the word 'on sight'.

nightingale	compare	describe	confuse
mistake	spoilsport	conversation	enquire
unforgettable	temperature	vicious	procession

Total	/12

Assessment L: Red Words

Ask the student to read these words 'on sight'.

does	tall	come	watch	who	were
brother	any	there	where	two	small
love	many	here	once	buy	worse
thought	talk	caught	bought	walk	could
anyone	would	great	son	water	should

Total	/30

Timetables 7

The timetables help you to organise the parallel implementation of the phonic work, and the *Module* lessons. (Set 1 of the phonic materials should be taught in its entirety before the *Modules* are begun.)

Two timetables (or sets of alternative timetables) are suggested:

- a timetable for the *Introductory Module*
  (four of the reading activities and one of the writing activities are included)
- a timetable for *Modules 1-33*
  (seven reading activities and three writing activities are included)
  The activities for each day lead up to the starred ☆ activity which is the main focus.

Timetable for the *Introductory Module*

Phonic knowledge required before starting the *Introductory Module:*

- the ability to read Speed Sounds Cards Set 1 at speed with correct pronunciation
- the ability to sound blend Green Words Set 1

Use this timetable for one or two stories/passages together. There are two parts to the lesson:

- the phonic lesson (5-10 minutes)
- the story/passage lesson (50 minutes)

Four of the nine reading activities and one of the nine writing activities are used at this stage.

Day 1 One or two stories each day	Handbook reference
Phonic lesson: *Revise Speed Sounds Set 1* *Teach Speed Sounds Set 2*	pp.17-32
Introductory Module lesson:	
Reading activity 1: Practise reading the Speed Sounds on page 2	p.43
Reading activity 2: Read the Green and Red Words	p.43
Reading activity 5: Read the story/passage ☆	p.46
Reading activity 6: Re-read the story/passage and discuss the 'questions to talk about'	p.47
Writing activity 5: Hold a sentence - these are given on page 26 of the *Introductory Module*	p.55

Timetable for *Modules 1-33*

Knowledge required before starting *Module 1:*

- the ability to read Speed Sounds Cards Set 1 at speed with correct pronunciation
- the ability to sound-blend Green Words Set 1
- the ability to read the *Introductory Module*

Knowledge required before starting *Module 4:*

- the ability to read Speed Sounds Cards Sets 1 and 2 at speed with correct pronunciation
- the ability to sound-blend Green Words Sets 1 and 2
- the ability to read *Module 3*

Knowledge required before starting *Module 15:*

- the ability to read Speed Sounds Cards Sets 1, 2 and 3 at speed with correct pronunciation
- the ability to sound-blend Green Words Sets 1, 2 and 3
- the ability to read *Module 14*

Let students progress with their reading, even if some have difficulty in spelling.

There are two parts to the lesson:

- the phonic lesson (5-10 minutes)
- the *Module* lesson (50–55 minutes)

Timetable for the *Modules* (continued)

Five-day plan

Follow the five-day plan if your students need to focus on reading as well as writing.

Day 1	Day 2	Day 3	Day 4	Day 5
Phonic lessons: Speed Sounds Sets 2/3 pp. 29–37	Phonic lessons: Speed Sounds Sets 2/3 pp. 29–37	Phonic lessons: Speed Sounds Sets 2/3 pp. 29–37		
Reading activity 1: Practise reading the Speed Sounds p. 43	Reading activity 1: Practise reading the Speed Sounds p. 43	Reading activity 1: Practise reading the Speed Sounds p. 43	Reading activity 9: Practise reading the Speed Words p. 49	Reading activity 9: Practise reading the Speed Words p. 49
Reading activity 2: Read the Green, Red and Challenge Words p. 43	Reading activity 2: Read the Green, Red and Challenge Words p. 43	Reading activity 9: Practise reading the Speed Words p. 49	Writing activity 9: Write a guided composition (Deconstruction) p. 58	Writing activity 8: Write a composition based on picture prompts or Writing activity 9: Write a guided composition pp. 57–58
Reading activity 3: Listen to the introduction p. 45	Reading activity 6: Re-read the story and discuss the 'questions to talk about' ☆ p. 47	Reading activity 7: Read the story with fluency and expression. ☆ p. 48		
Reading activity 4: Discuss the vocabulary check p. 45	Reading activity 8: Answer the 'questions to read and answer' p. 49	Writing activity 4: Take a spelling test p. 55		
Reading activity 5: Read the story ☆ p. 46	Writing activity 2: Play 'sound-grapheme fingers' p. 53	Writing activity 6: Build a sentence p. 56		
Writing activity 1: Play 'sound-grapheme rhythms' p. 52	Writing activity 3: Carry out a spelling check p. 54	Writing activity 7: Edit for spelling/ punctuation/ grammar p. 56		
Writing activity 2: Play 'sound-grapheme fingers' p. 53	Writing activity 5: Hold a sentence p. 55			

Timetable for the *Modules* (continued)

Four-day plan

Follow the four-day plan if your students need to focus mainly on writing.
If Day 1 is Monday, the new Day 1 for the next module will be Friday.

Day 1	Day 2	Day 3	Day 4
Phonic lessons: Speed Sounds Set 3 pp. 33–37	Phonic lessons: Speed Sounds Set 3 pp. 33–37		
Reading activity 1: Practise reading the Speed Sounds p. 43	Reading activity 6: Re-read the story and discuss the 'questions to talk about' p. 47	Reading activity 9: Practise reading the Speed Words p. 49	Writing activity 8: Write a composition based on picture prompts or Writing activity 9: Write a guided composition ☆ pp. 57–58
Reading activity 2: Read the Green, Red and Challenge Words p. 43	Reading activity 8: Answer the 'questions to read and answer' p. 49	Writing activity 4: Take a spelling test p. 55	
Reading activity 3: Listen to the introduction p. 45	Writing activity 3: Carry out a spelling check p. 54	Writing activity 8: Write a composition based on picture prompts or Writing activity 9: Write a guided composition (Deconstruction) ☆ pp. 57–58	
Reading activity 4: Discuss the vocabulary check ☆ p. 45	Writing activity 5: Hold a sentence ☆ p. 55		
Reading activity 5: Read the story p. 46	Writing activity 6: Build a sentence p. 56		
Writing activity 1: Play 'sound-grapheme rhythms' p. 52	Writing activity 7: Edit for spelling/ punctuation/ grammar p. 56		
Writing activity 2: Play 'sound-grapheme fingers' p. 53			

Appendix A - Speed Sounds chart

Consonants: *stretch*

f	l	m	n	r	s	v	z	sh	th	ng
ff	ll	mm	nn	rr	ss	ve	zz	ti		nk
ph	le	mb	kn	wr	se		s	ci		
					c					
					ce					
	✓	✓	✓	✓		✓	✓			✓

Consonants: *bounce*

b	c	d	g	h	j	p	qu	t	w	x	y	ch
bb	k	dd	gg		g	pp		tt	wh			tch
	ck				ge							
	ch											
✓		✓	✓		✓		✓		✓		✓	

✓ = *'singable', voiced consonant sounds*

Vowels

a	e	i	o	u	ay	ee	igh	ow
	ea				a-e	y	i-e	o-e
					ai	ea	ie	oa
						e	i	o

oo	*oo*	ar	or	air	ir	ou	oy	ire	ear	ure
u-e			oor	are	ur	ow	oi			
ue			ore		er					
ew			aw							
			au							

Appendix B - Red Words used in the *Modules*

Display the Red Words on a Red Word Wall as soon as it has been introduced in the story. These words contain graphemes that are not on the chart representing the sound in these words. The shaded part tells you the 'grotty' grapheme, that is not listed on the grapheme chart.

I the you your said was are of want what they

to do does all call tall small any many anyone

some come watch who where there here were

brother other mother father love above two once buy

worse walk talk caught bought thought through

wear whole could would should great son water

Red 'for a while' words

These include graphemes that have not been taught when they are needed in the reading books. As soon as the grapheme has been taught, these turn into Green Words!

he me we she be no so go old her saw my

by why now how down over school

Appendix C - *Read Write Inc. Fresh Start* and the KS2 English SATs

The chart below shows how *Fresh Start* develops the reading skills assessed in the KS2 English SATs.

Assessment focuses for reading
Pupil's ability to:

1. Use a range of strategies, including accurate decoding of text, to read for meaning.	*Fresh Start* teaches accurate decoding of text to read for meaning. Pupils learn to read effortlessly so they can put all their energy into comprehending what they read.
2. Understand, describe, select or retrieve information, events or ideas from texts and use quotation and reference to text.	*Fresh Start Modules* have 'Questions to talk about' after the text. They are a mix of: • Find it' questions, whereby pupils select or retrieve information from the text, and • 'Prove it' questions, whereby pupils use quotation and reference to the text to give evidence and/or explain. Also p. 8 of each *Module* has a text which is used for deconstruction, whereby pupils look at the content, style and structure of the text.
3. Deduce, infer or interpret information, events or ideas from texts.	'Questions to read and answer' after the text provide practice for pupils to deduce, infer or interpret information, events or ideas from texts, e.g. see *Module 24* p. 7.
4. Identify and comment on the structure and organisation of texts, including grammatical and presentational features at text level.	'Questions to talk about' and 'Questions to read and answer' after the text often require pupils to do this, e.g. p. 7 *Module 21* 'Questions to talk about' (good look at structure). Also often looked at in the p. 8 text, e.g. *Module 21* 'Why didn't the writer start with this paragraph?' Also p. 7 *Module 17* 2nd 'Find it' question and the 'Prove it' question.
5. Explain and comment on writer's use of language, including grammatical and literary features at word and sentence level.	'Prove it' questions often ask pupils to explain and comment on writer's use of language, e.g. p. 7 *Module 17* and 1st, 3rd and 4th 'Find it' questions. Also often looked at in the p. 8 text, e.g. *Module 21* 'This paragraph is about how the narrator feels. Underline what makes it effective.'
6. Identify and comment on writer's purposes and viewpoints, and the overall effect of the text on the reader.	'Questions to talk about' often require pupils to do this, e.g. p. 7 *Module 17* 2nd 'Find it' question. Also p. 7 *Module 24* 'Prove it' question, 3rd 'Question to read and answer'. Also often looked at in the p. 8 text, e.g. *Module 24* 'What is the purpose of each paragraph?' and *Module 21* 'How does this opening paragraph grab your attention?'
7. Relate texts to their social, cultural and historical contexts and literary traditions.	See p. 7 *Module 17* or p. 8 *Module 24.*

Appendix C - *Read Write Inc. Fresh Start* and the KS2 English SATs

The chart below shows how *Fresh Start* develops the writing skills assessed in the KS2 English SATs.

Assessment focuses for writing
Pupil's ability to:

1. Write imaginative, interesting and thoughtful texts.	*Fresh Start* provides good models of imaginative, interesting and thoughtful texts and develops pupils' writing skills, vocabulary and grammar so they can produce similar texts. The 'Build a sentence' activity develops pupils' vocabulary as they build an idea into an interesting sentence. The deconstruction texts on p. 8 provide models for the pupils' own writing in the guided compositions within a writing frame.
2. Produce texts which are appropriate to task, reader and purpose.	The deconstruction texts on p. 8 of the *Modules* look at the sequencing and structure of a model text, before pupils write their own texts. The guided compositions ensure pupils have a scaffold for their writing, to produce well structured, cohesive texts, e.g. p. 9 *Module 24*. This scaffolding is reduced in some of the later *Modules*.
3. Organise and present whole texts effectively, sequencing and structuring information, ideas and events.	
4. Construct paragraphs and use cohesion within and between paragraphs.	
5. Vary sentences for clarity, purpose and effect.	The deconstruction texts on p. 8 of the *Modules* look at the style of a model text, before pupils write their own texts. The 'Build a sentence' activity teaches pupils to produce effective sentences.
6. Write with technical accuracy of syntax and punctuation in phrases, clauses and sentences.	Many of the *Modules* have syntax activities, e.g. p. 11 Edit 2 *Module 17.* Punctuation is often focused on in Edit 1, e.g. p. 10 *Module 24.*
7. Select appropriate and effective vocabulary.	Many of the *Modules* have activities requiring pupils to select the most appropriate vocabulary, e.g. p. 11 *Module 21* and *Module 24.*
8. Use correct spelling.	*Fresh Start Modules* all contain a number of spelling activities, including: • spelling multi-syllabic words • spelling words with irregular spelling • finding speling errors in a text. Pupils learn to spell effortlessly so they can put all their energy into composing what they write.
Handwriting	Pupils are taught the correct letter formation of all the letters when they learn the Speed Sounds.
Genre and text type coverage	Information texts, reports, non-chronological reports, recounts, instructions, explanation texts, adverts, recipes, biographies, re-tellings of Shakespeare *(Macbeth, Romeo and Juliet),* writing in the first and third person, stories with familiar settings, letters, historical stories *(Jason and the Argonauts),* humorous stories, rhyme, stories from other cultures.

We learn

10% of what we read

20% of what we hear

30% of what we see

50% of what we both see and hear

70% of what is discussed with others

85% of what we experience personally

95% of what we teach to someone else

William Glasser

Appendix E - Charts to develop

Good partners:

Look	Sound	Feel
Sit side-by-side Always return the stop signal TTYP quickly after question has been asked Take turns in answering first Wait while another is talking	Are helpful to each other Check that they both understand the question Talk loudly enough for their partner to hear, though not too loudly to interrupt others Build on what their partner says Say '*We* think that ...' if asked to report back	Ready to answer Safe and secure Listen to each other Are interested in what each other has to say

Appendix E - Charts to develop

Positive teaching chart: *Develop a similar chart with your staff. Identify specific behaviour that makes a positive teacher.*

A positive teacher:

Looks	***Sounds*** ***(says things like)***	***Feels***
Smiles a lot Uses eye contact Takes a student to one side to discuss negative behaviour Uses students' names	You will soon be able to ... This is hard at the moment but you will soon be able to do it Which part do you think I need to explain more? Thank you for that answer	Relaxed Enthusiastic Well prepared

Appendix E - Charts to develop

Negative teaching chart: *Develop a similar chart with staff. This may sound a negative task, but is actually very amusing ... if a little cringe-making!*

A negative teacher:

Looks	***Sounds*** ***(says things like)***	***Feels***
Frowns a lot	I'm waiting	Tense
Uses little eye contact	If you do that again ...	Fed up
	How can I carry on?	Poorly prepared
	This is the last time I'm going to tell you	
	If I hear that one more time	
	How many times have I asked you to ...?	
	Shouts/nags/shushes	

Appendix F - Introductory partner games

These are useful for getting the students used to working in pairs. The nature of the games will depend on the age of the students.

Start a '*partnership pack*' - this can be added to as teachers develop and refine the partner work.

Five things I know about my partner

The students find out and remember five facts about their partners.

They can then introduce their partners using this information:

'My partner's name is ...

He/she lives at ...

He/she's got a brother called ...

and a cat called ...

and he/she likes watching 'Eastenders'.

Extend this format with older students.

Appendix F - Introductory partner games

Animal fact file

Give out animal (or transport/clothing/toy) cards. Partners prepare three sentences about their animal, for example:

'This animal is furry.

This animal is white.

This animal likes human beings.'

One partner is chosen to speak (do not let them know who this is going to be until the last minute). The rest of the class have to guess the animal.

Silent drawing

Give each partnership one piece of paper and one pencil. Tell them they are going to draw a fish/animal/house/monster, but this must be done in silence.

Every ten seconds, say 'Stop.' The students then give the pencils to their partners, and the partners extend the drawings.

When you have done this a few times, ask the partners to describe their drawings to each other.

The house

Partners discuss a plan for a house to suit a person who wants to live underground/in a tree/in a train /in the most perfect house in the world.

When they are ready, they draw the house in silence, taking turns as above.

To and fro

Partners take turns to speak. They could count backwards or forwards in twos, threes or fives, or say a well-known rhyme in alternate words/lines.

They could teach each other a short poem or rhyme.

Appendix G - Gathering responses from partner discussion

There are various ways of gathering responses.

Some students are very nervous about feeding back in front of the whole class. This will need to be handled sensitively, with shy students being gently encouraged to speak out.

Don't revert to 'hands up'. This will have a detrimental effect on partner work, as some students will stop putting any effort into discussion if they think the usual volunteers will report back.

Avoid asking students to report back to their partners' answers, especially if personal, individual responses were required. If a student is busy remembering their own idea, they may not remember their partner's. When partner work is well developed, partners start their response with either 'We think that ...' or 'I think ... but my partner thinks ...'

Number 1s or Number 2s

Say: 'I'm going to choose a few Number 1s (or 2s) to report back.' Only choose a few, as students easily get bored when they are just listening.

You may want to alert the partners who are going to feed back, or you may choose not to give them any warning. If you alert students too early, the ones who are not chosen may stop making an effort. Change the 'starters' randomly. This prevents a situation in which one student dominates or another opts out. Some students almost burst with their answers, whereas others say, 'What do you think?' (Not because they are being polite, but because they prefer their partners to do the work!)

Build on one

Warn one student from one partnership that they will report back. Tell the students that you will ask the rest to build on their answer.

Tell another partner

Only use this if the students can organise themselves quickly, without fuss.

Each Number 1 tells another Number 1, and each Number 2 tells another Number 2.

Appendix G - Gathering responses from partner discussion

All together

Ask the students to answer after you have counted to three. This is a useful strategy when you predict that they will all give the same one-word answer.

Round the clock

If the students have been asked a question such as 'Can you tell me the names of all the colours in the world?' and the partners have had time to talk, ask them all to call out their answers as you listen and draw a clock in the air. They must try to find spaces to call out, not too loudly, in between other students' answers. It should sound like popcorn cooking!

Signals

If the question has two obvious answers, ask the students to put their forefingers on their heads if they think one thing, and on their knees if they think the other.

Yes or no

Repeat one student's response, and ask the others to put their thumbs up if they agree and their thumbs down if they disagree. Ask them for their reasons.

Teacher feedback

Listen in carefully to a few discussions, and report the partners' ideas back to them. This is useful if you want to:

- gather the most helpful answers
- gather answers from students who are finding it difficult to articulate them clearly (this will give a voice to less able students who have not been listened to before)
- gather answers from shy students, who will begin to acquire a voice through you.

If you find that most students are giving the same answer, say 'I heard nearly everyone say ... Did anyone have a different answer?' This will allow you to move the lesson on.

Appendix H - Modules genre coverage chart

Title	Reading Text	Writing Deconstruction	Writing
1. The Thing from the Black Planet	Fiction	Description of a creature	Picture strip based on text read
2. A wolf cub	Fiction	First person recount	Picture strip based on text read
3. Big Malc	Fiction	Wanted poster	Picture strip based on text read
4. Hay into gold	Fiction - Rumplestiltskin	Alternative version Rumplestiltskin	Picture strip based on text read
5. Keeping a cat	Non Fiction - Information	Report - stick insects	Picture strip based on text read
6. Bill Bright's fishing trip	Fiction	Letter	Picture strip based on text read
7. The yellow light	Fiction	Poem	Picture strip based on text read
8. Baboons on the loose	Fiction	Newspaper report	Picture strip based on text read
9. Bart the champ	Fiction	Newspaper report	Picture strip based on text read
10. Lorna	Fiction	Story continuation	Picture strip based on text read
11. A bad hair day	Fiction	Letter of complaint	Picture strip based on text read
12. A good win for the red shirts	Non Fiction - Newspaper report	First person recount	Picture strip based on text read
13. A player to be proud of	Non Fiction - Biography David Beckham	Biography	Picture strip based on text read
14. Cook and Enjoy	Non Fiction Recipe instructions	Recount - How to make pancakes	Instructions: How to access the Internet
15. Late	Fiction	Letter of apology	Letter of apology
16. The weaving contest	Fiction - Greek myth	Descriptive recount first person	Descriptive recount first person
17. Celia Smith's quick goldfish pie	Non Fiction - Humorous recipe	Recipe	Recipe for disgusting sandwiches
18. Beep!	Fiction	Discursive text - pros and cons of uniform	Discursive - pros and cons of detentions
19. Spellbound	Non Fiction - First person recount/dialogue	Play script	Play script
20. The Outlaws	Fiction	Diary entry	Diary entry
21. Romeo and Juliet	Fiction	Recount of events	Continuation of recount
22. Sunburst Teen Magazine	Non Fiction - Magazine problem page	Problem page letter - problem/answer	Write answer to page letter
23. How does it feel to be an astronaut?	Non Fiction - Information	Persuasive text	Persuasive article for school magazine
24. Raiders of the lost shark	Non Fiction - Email complaint correspondence	Letter of complaint	Letter of complaint
25. Jason's quest	Fiction - Greek myth	Diary entry	Diary entry
26. New boy	Non Fiction - First person recount	Witness report	Witness report
27. Kevin the killer hamster	Fiction	Description of being lost	Description of being lost
28. Il Bello	Non Fiction - Account of horse race	Letter describing race events	Continuation of letter
29. Emergency	Non Fiction - first aid guidance	Fire policy	Fire policy for school
30. Creature	Non Fiction - First person recount	Instructions	Instructions
31. Macbeth	Fiction	Descriptive scene setting	Descriptive scene setting
32. The invisible city	Non Fiction - Account eruption of Mt Vesuvius	Newspaper report	Newspaper report
33. Penalty for piracy: Execution	Non Fiction - Biography	Advertisement	Advertisement

Appendix I - Before you start: Activities for teachers

The six activities below will prepare you for teaching the programme. Work through them, preferably with a friend so that you can help each other as you practise.

Terminology

In *Read Write Inc. Fresh Start*, the word 'sound' means 'the smallest unit of sound that we can hear or speak'. The word 'grapheme' indicates the written version of the sound.

c-a-t	= 3 sounds and 3 graphemes
ch-a-t	= 3 sounds and 3 graphemes
l-igh-t	= 3 sounds and 3 graphemes
c-r-a-sh	= 4 sounds and 4 graphemes
s-t-r-ee-t	= 5 sounds and 5 graphemes

'Green Words' are words made from the high-frequency graphemes shown on the *Read Write Inc. Fresh Start* Speed Sounds Poster. A grapheme can only be used to make up a Green Word when it has been taught from the poster.

'Red Words' are common words that contain low-frequency graphemes not included on the poster, e.g. 's**ai**d', 'w**a**nt', 'r**ough**', 'thr**ough**', 'w**oul**d', 'd**augh**ter', 'b**a**ll', 'w**al**k'.

Some common words are designated 'red for a while' – red until the grapheme has been taught, e.g. 'go', 'so', 'he', 'we'. These words are starred on the Red Word cards.

Sound Talk

Teachers need to know how to speak any single-syllabic word in pure sounds.

So: c-a-t = cat (say 'c' 'a' 't' *not* 'cuh' 'a' 'tuh')

Appendix I - Before you start: Activities for teachers

Activity 1: Learn to say the 44 sounds

- **Consonant sounds**

Stretchy consonant sounds

Practise stretching each sound. (Avoid saying 'fuh', 'luh', 'muh', 'nuh', etc.)

ffff	llll	mmmm	nnnn	rrrr	ssss	vvvv	zzzz	ssshhh	ttthhh	nnng (thi**ng**)

Now say the shortest sound you can without an 'uh'!

f	l	m	n	r	s	v	z	sh	th	ng

The unvoiced 'th' sound is used in the first set of phonic lessons.

Bouncy consonant sounds

Practise 'bouncing' each sound. (Avoid saying 'cuh', 'puh', 'tuh', 'chuh'.)

c-c-c-c k-k-k-k	h-h-h-h	p-p-p-p	t-t-t-t	ch-ch-ch-ch

Now say the shortest sound you can without an 'uh'!

c	h	p	t	ch

These are also 'bouncy' sounds, but it is harder not to say 'uh' – just do your best!
Practise bouncing each sound.

b-b-b-b	d-d-d-d	g-g-g-g	j-j-j-j	w-w-w-w	y-y-y-y

Now say the shortest sound you can without an 'uh'!

b	d	g	j	w	y

Double consonant sounds

These sounds are actually two sounds made closely together, but they are counted as one.

x (c s)	qu (c w)	nk (ng k)

(nk is paired with ng on the Speed Sounds Poster)

Appendix I - Before you start: Activities for teachers

Vowel sounds

The English language can be confusing, because there are only five vowel letters ('a', 'e', 'i', 'o', 'u') but twenty vowel sounds.

Practise saying each vowel sound in the accent used in your region.

a apple	e egg	i insect	o orange	u umbrella	ay day	ee see	igh high	ow blow

oo zoo	oo book	ar car	or for	air fair	ir girl	ou shout	oy boy	ire fire	ear hear	ure pure

Now practise saying all 44 sounds.

Activity 2: Learn to say words in Sound Talk

As a *Read Write Inc. Fresh Start* teacher, you will need to be able to say any single-syllable word in Sound Talk so that the students can learn to blend the sounds into a word.

The words in each of the rows below share a vowel sound, but may contain different vowel graphemes. Ask someone to say each word for you so you are not tempted to focus on the spelling. Say the vowel sound first, and then say the word in Sound Talk. Touch a finger as you say each sound.

The number of sounds is printed after each word.

a	c-a-t 3	f-a-t 3	m-a-sh 3	s-p-l-a-sh 5
e	h-e-n 3	h-e-l-p 4	h-ea-d 3	b-r-ea-d 4
i	p-i-n 3	th-i-n 3	th-i-ng 3	th-i-nk 3
o	l-o-t 3	l-o-ng 3	l-o-s-t 4	p-o-n-d 4
u	h-u-t 3	j-u-m-p 4	c-r-u-s-t 5	j-u-s-t 4

Appendix I - Before you start: Activities for teachers

ay	d-ay 2	m-a-k(e) 3	t-r-ai-n 4	
ee	g-r-ee-n 4	t-ea 2	h-e 2	k-ey 2
igh	n-igh-t 3	b-i-k(e) 3	t-ie 2	f-i-n-d 4
ow	s-n-ow 3	h-o-m(e) 3	g-oa-t 3	n-o 2
oo	z-oo 2	b-r-u-t(e) 4	b-l-ue 3	ch-ew 2
ar	sh-ar-k 3			
or	f-or 2	d-oor 2	s-n-ore 3	j-aw 2
air	s-t-air 3	c-are 2		
ir	g-ir-l 3	n-ur-se 3	h-er 2	
ou	ou-t 2	t-ow-n 3		
oi	b-oy 2	s-p-oi-l 4		
ire	f-ire 2			
ear	h-ear 2			
ure	p-ure 2			

More practice...

h-ea-d 3, ar-m 2, l-e-g 3, b-a-ck 3, n-e-ck 3, t-u-m 3,
sh-oe 2, z-i-p 3, v-e-s-t 4, s-o-ck 3, c-oa-t 3, h-oo-d 3,
r-e-d 3, b-l-ue 3, g-r-ee-n 4, b-l-a-ck 4, p-ai-n-t 4, p-e-n 3, c-u-p 3,
r-u-n 3, s-k-i-p 4, j-u-m-p 4, w-al-k 3 (or), th-i-nk 3, s-m-i-l(e) 4, s-i-t 3,
s-t-a-n-d 5, l-u-n-ch 4, t-ea 2, b-r-ea-k 4, h-o-m(e) 3, ch-air 2, l-igh-t 3,
w-a-ll 3 (or), t-oy 2, b-oo-k 3, b-a-g 3, kn-i-f(e) 3, f-or-k 3,
s-p-oo-n 4, d-i-sh 3, p-l-a-t(e) 4, p-a-n 3, b-r-ea-d 4, j-a-m 3,
c-a-k(e) 3, t-oa-s-t 4, s-ou-p 3, h-a-m 3, ch-ee-se 3, l-oo 2, s-i-nk 3,
s-oa-p 3, m-a-t 3, t-a-p 3, f-l-oor 3, d-u-ck 3, s-p-l-a-sh 5,
s-a-d 3, c-r-o-ss 4, g-o 2, p-l-ea-se 4, m-a-d 3, g-l-a-d 4

Appendix I - Before you start: Activities for teachers

Activity 3: Understand the Speed Sounds Poster

In each sound box on the poster there is one sound but usually more than one grapheme.

Complete the chart below by adding the graphemes printed in bold in the following words. (The first two have been completed for you.)

- **Consonant sounds**

photo bell funny stuff puddle wrap know horse carry circus piece give buzz caution hobble stick chemist giggle bridge barge gentle topple when little catch delicious

- **Vowel sounds**

my tie boat kind flew saw door no blue burn her coin Paul snore brown make bike home brute happy she

- **Consonant sounds**

f ph	l ll	m	n	r	s	v	z	sh	th	ng nk

b	c k	d	g	h	j	p	qu	t	w	x	y	ch

- **Vowel sounds**

a	e	i	o	u	ay	ee	igh	ow

oo	*oo*	ar	or	air	ir	ou	oy	ire	ear	ure

Appendix I - Before you start: Activities for teachers

Activity 4: Check what you have learned about sounds and graphemes

Look at the words below.
Draw a dot under each one-letter grapheme.
Draw a line under each two- or three-letter grapheme.
Draw an arc to join each 'split grapheme' ('a-e', 'i-e', 'o-e', 'u-e').

e.g. p l ay sh ake

am and bad blot plan crib camp wind pond desk blend

grunt twist stiff press bluff thing spring drink splash

clutch slump stretch spray new boat tooth care stair

door make spark sprain brute bird spike law flight hair

need join out read furl bloke floor stone tie brown

bow joy fire hear pure

Activity 5: Read in syllables

Read the words below in syllables. Say each syllable as it looks, not as it is pronounced, e.g. '**Mon**/day', 'choc/o/**late**', 'pic/**ture**' (as in 'pure').

Mon/day choc/o/late des/troy pic/ture pill/ow chil/dren

con/cen/trate sta/tion pa/tience temp/er/a/ture ac/cep/tance

Appendix I - Before you start: Activities for teachers

Activity 6: Count the graphemes in words with more than one syllable

Look at the words below.
Say each syllable as it looks, not as it is pronounced.
Draw a dot under each one-letter grapheme.
Draw a line under each two- or three-letter grapheme.
Draw an arc to join each 'split grapheme'.

fo/llow con/cen/trate de/cide a/lone re/cog/nise bo/rrow

be/have a/mount croc/o/dile ex/tra/va/gant ac/cep/tance

dis/a/ppoint com/pare im/pa/tience dis/grace/ful be/cause

aw/ful de/li/cious ac/tion